**Instead of just *doing* time,
they're doing something *with* it!**

OVER THE WALL is our offering to you, an attempt to show the other side of the coin, some sensitivity in place of the much publicized brutality, a bit of humor in place of the usual prison ugliness. Perhaps the entire book might not be your cup of tea, but we hope that somewhere in these pages is a little something for everyone; in these pages is a little something for everyone; enjoyment for those who seek entertainment, enlightenment for those who seek perception. . . ."

THE EDITORS

OVER THE WALL

EDITED BY

Frank Earl Andrews *and* Albert Dickens

PYRAMID BOOKS · NEW YORK

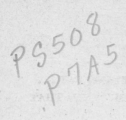

OVER THE WALL

A PYRAMID BOOK

Copyright © 1974 by Frank Earl Andrews and Albert Dickens
All rights reserved. No part of this book may be reproduced in any
form or by any electronic or mechanical means including information storage and retrieval systems without permission in writing
from the Publisher, except by a reviewer who may quote brief
passages in a review.

Pyramid edition published November 1974

ISBN 0-515-03513-0

Library of Congress Catalog Card Number: 74-6509

Printed in the United States of America

Pyramid Books are published by Pyramid Communications, Inc.
Its trademarks, consisting of the word "Pyramid" and the portrayal
of a pyramid, are registered in the United States Patent Office.

Pyramid Communications, Inc., 919 Third Avenue,
New York, N.Y. 10022

TO ... LESLIE AND PAT ...
BECAUSE THEY MAKE ME FEEL THAT WAY ...

I Stole a Lilac

Norman A. Porter

Alas for poor rehabilitation
and all her promises
either talked or tried
of redeeming convicts
by making them socially fit
for tonight
I stole a Lilac.

I stole a Lilac
a sweet smelling flower
that tickled my nose
and sent traces of nature
burning through every nerve
alas for poor rehabilitation
and all her promises.

CONTENTS

Introduction

Over the Wall is a compilation of essays and short fiction written by men and women incarcerated in prisons and reformatories around the country. *Over the Wall* is the culmination of human effort from people, who would like to show something behind the walls and fences, besides Attica 71, Rahway's Thanksgiving riot, or the recent events at Walpole, McAlester, Trenton State Prison and San Quentin.

The institutions represented here are located in various parts of the United States and in some cases it was necessary to communicate through an outside address, due to restrictions on interinstitutional correspondence. We would like to extend heartfelt thanks to those solid-gold folks out there in the free, who acted as our eyes, ears and legs, because without them we would never have gotten off the ground, as there are no federal or state programs designed to assist prisoners who wish to do things themselves. Funds are allocated only for projects recommended by "expert criminology" panels, whose members know as much about the minds and hearts of prisoners as a polar bear does about flying.

Efforts came in various forms and in one instance, crudely written on pieces of a brown paper bag. Sometimes determined prisoners found their way to us with "inmate papers," institutional publications that are censored by the respective prison administrations. The talent stuck out anyway, like the nose cone on an Apollo moon rocket.

Over the Wall is our offering to you, an attempt to show the other side of the coin, some sensitivity in place of the much publicized brutality, a bit of humor in place of the usual prison ugliness.

Perhaps the entire book might not be your cup of tea, but we hope that somewhere in these pages is a little something for everyone; enjoyment for those who seek entertainment, enlightenment for those who seek perception. If so, let us know—and fasten your seat belts, because we haven't even scraped the surface yet.

OVER THE WALL

ROBERT E. CHINN

Rahway State Prison, Rahway, New Jersey

Bobby Chinn, a drug addict since 1948, has spent over half of his life behind bars. He was born in Newark, New Jersey, and is currently serving a twenty-two- to thirty-eight-year sentence. He is an accomplished trombonist, composer/arranger, and knows just about everything there is to know about the printing profession. He is presently engaged in the writing of his autobiography; a smidgen of it is his contribution here.

Daymare*

Robert E. Chinn

School. White people. What's happenin' with white people? Where do they come from? Is God white? Why do they want to own everythin'? Do they own me? They have a funny odor—why? Vampire werewolves! I see a vast wilderness covered with snow, large packs of ferocious gray and white wolves. Some white people are comin'! The wolf packs are separatin' into two groups; young and mature. The mature wolves of one pack are attackin' the mature wolves of another pack. Many wolves are killed. The white people make a funny sound. The wolves stop fightin' and are now lyin' amidst the white people. The white people let the wolves bite them and suck their blood. The young wolves watch and whine. Slowly the mature wolves turn into white people! After all the wolves were changed and clothed, the white people made another funny sound. The young werewolves are now eatin' the carcasses of the wolves that were killed in battle. The old and new white people are goin' away. As they walk away, I know that in order for them to

* This and the selections that follow are excerpted from *How Many Times Must I Die?*

17

remain white people, they need blood—human blood! The old white people gave the mature wolves just enough of their enriched blood to make the transformation and to hold them until they captured their own victims.

Are all white people vampire werewol . . . ?

"Robert!"

School. Classroom. Children. The Teacher . . . .

"Robert, you were daydreaming, weren't you? Are you sick? Are you cold? Why are you trembling? Let's go and see the nurse."

I stared at her for a moment, stood up, then walked out of the classroom.

"Robert, wait for me in the hall!"

She caught up with me. "Robert. Robert!"

I turned my head just in time to see her grab at me. I dodged.

"Robert! I'm not going to BITE you! Wait! Rob. . . . Don't run. . . ."

Like the generation before us, my comrades and I emerged from the back yards of Rutgers Street to emulate the big boys at school, the playground, the movies, jitterbugging in the storefronts, dances and to take our turn sitting on the stoops close to the bars and corners, telling lies, catcalling, cajoling girls and plotting stratagems for our future campaigns: crashing parties, poolrooms and bars.

Predator or Prey

Robert E. Chinn

. . . . Early one autumn morning, a thousand years ago, while asleep on a pallet in the back of a furniture truck that parked regularly in a gas station/garage on the corner of 13th Avenue and Wallace Street, I was jolted awake by the sound of a starting car. It was the morning after the party. . . .

I was struggling with a very serious problem when I met Luther: how to make myself look eighteen so I could go into, and stay in, the neighborhood poolroom. Luther, my senior by eight years, after noticing me peeping in the poolroom window a few times, started waving at me. Then, when he saw me hanging around outside all the time, he would come out and explain the game to me. He turned out to be the answer to my problem: the owner, Rubin, and Luther were good friends (wine buddies) and if the poolroom was crowded, Rubin did not say anything if I came in with Luther. Soon I was running errands and racking balls. Rubin was once the New Jersey billiards champion and he and Luther taught me everything they knew about pool. Luther introduced me to reefers and benzedrine.

. . . . He had taken me to his cousin's house party.

There he gave me beer, wine, whiskey and three or four reefers, one right after the other. Someone started shaking the house . . . ? I felt my way to the door. "Hey, Chinn," he called. "What's happenin', man? Oh, dig that cat. He's stoned! Where're you goin'? Dig. There's a black Buick right in front of the house; it's my cousin's. Get in the back seat and sleep off some of that head." The car found me, opened its door; I climbed in and curled up on the back seat. . . .

Luther was a hustler. Every time I went downtown with him, I learned something new. His credentials were impeccable—City Home, Jamesburg, Rahway, Caldwell, Trenton State Prison.

. . . . The world had exploded! I was hurled into deep space. Stars! I must find a way to avoid hitting a star. "Hey, are you asleep?" A voice, but I don't see anyone. I'm all alone, just me and the stars. It's cold. Someone is lying very close to me . . . ? It's a man . . . ? He's trying to unbuckle my belt . . . ? Why? He's very close to me . . . ? He's hard . . . ? Hard!? I have to throw up! I belched, reached for the door, opened it, jumped out and slammed it behind me. I ran and vomited. . . .

Luther was more than a damned good pool shooter. He was an expert con man, mugger, drunk roller, creeper (sneak thief), pickpocket, car jimmier, baggage lifter, gambler, shoplifter, and . . . an asshole bandit!

House Stole A Red Bike

Robert E. Chinn

"Seemore?" (See more scalp than hair.)

"Yeah."

"Who's next?"

"Me!" said Rock, pointing at himself. "I helped git her down here."

"Me!" Ken said. "I hollered second."

"Me!" House insisted. "She said me!"

"Me!" Red cried. "I got her down here the last time."

"If Mr. Freeman hears us, ain't nobody goin' next," Ghost cautioned.

"Why he so slow?" Rock asked impatiently, then went and peeped into the bin.

"You slow too," said House, looking at Ken. "You be talkin' and kissin'."

"I'm faster'n you!" Ken declared indignantly.

Red told Rock that he only wanted to peep, but he went into the bin. Shipwreck came out smiling.

"Red! I'm next. Okay. Okay. I'll fix you next time," Rock protested.

"You're scared of him," House needled. "Why you let him go next?"

"You goin' last," Rock said, looking hard at House.

"Why?" asked House.

"'Cause."

"'Cause what?"

" 'Cause you know what happened the last time," Rock said.

"Oh, no! She stopped 'cause she was hurtin'," House insisted.

"She stopped 'cause she don't like you," Rock shot back. So you go last."

House pointed at Ken. "He should go last."

"Why should I go last?" Ken asked.

"She likes you," House replied. "She'll lay there and let us all do it to her, just waitin' for you."

Ken shook his head. "Uh-uh!"

"Shhhh, somebody's comin'!" House whispered. "Y'all hide. I'll go and tell them to keep quiet." He tiptoed into the bin. Red came out buttoning his fly.

"Hide, Red, somebody's comin'!" Ghost warned softly from his hiding place. "Didn't House tell you?"

"He didn't tell me nothin'. He jus' told y'all that so he could go next. I don't know about House, Ken. She told him she's hurtin'. You better go talk to her."

Ken went in. House came out.

"I told you!" Rock said angrily.

"Rock, when you do it to her, tell her to let me do it, huh?" House pleaded. He put his hand in his pocket and started playing pocket pool.

"Uh-uh! Ask Ghost," Rock said, passing the buck. "She likes him better than me."

"I told you to stop callin' her Seemore," Ghost said. "She don't like that name."

"Okay," House said. "I won't call her Seemore anymore and I'll go last if you promise to tell her to let me do it to her."

"Okay," Ghost said, "if you promise to let me ride that red bike you stole. . . ."

22

Warm Turkey

Robert E. Chinn

Lying in bed, gowned and propped, I observed that the psychiatric ward was in the basement and you had to stand on a chair to look out of the window. I counted twenty-eight beds with patients in them; two beds were empty. As my eyes scanned clockwise from patient to patient, I realized that I was their current curiosity also. My gaze lingered on two patients: one wore leather cuffs on his ankles which were connected to a thick strap that was secured to the foot of the bed. The other was secured to the bed by both his ankles and his wrists.

"They're winos in d.t.'s," the wasted, pale man in the bed next to mine said. "They're going to strap you down too." He pointed to a white index card that was taped to the wall above the head of my bed.

The word *psycho* was printed on the card. I looked at his card. It had the same word on it, plus *V.A.*

"Veteran's Administration," he decoded. "I was in the army. During the Normandy invasion, me and a German bullet met while we were searching for the same thing—a place to hole up. Dig it?"

I smiled. "My name is Bob. What's your name?"

"Nick. When I was in the army hospital, I got hooked on morphine. You're on junk; I saw your tracks. You ever kick before?"

"Yeah, cold turkey, about two years ago. What do they give you here to ease the withdrawal?"

He laughed. "Are you kidding! They don't know how to treat heroin addiction. I've been in this ward twice, and I've seen about a dozen junkies kick here. I've only seen one guy get some medication, and that was a shot of morphine, after he went into a coma. He came close to not making it; that guy was really strung out! Don't worry. I'll keep an eye on you. I . . . here comes the goon. Let him strap one leg and one arm. If he tells you that his orders are to strap both your arms and legs, tell him you want to see the nurse. Drug addicts are only supposed to be strapped one and one. Got that?"

I nodded.

When the orderly put cuffs on both my ankles, I told him that I wanted to see the nurse, and why. He left and came back with a plump, middle-aged nurse who made a swishing sound as she walked. She took my pulse and felt my forehead.

"How are we doing, Robert?" she asked cheerfully.

"I feel all right now. My system is loaded and I don't expect my habit to come down until tomorrow mornin'. When it comes down, I'm goin' to vomit, urinate and my bowels are goin' to break. How am I goin' to use the bedpan if I'm strapped down?"

"The doctor wants you to stay in bed. We're only going to strap one arm and one leg."

I pointed to my cuffed ankles. She looked icily at the strapper. "If you promise to stay in bed, I won't strap you down until just before I go off duty at twelve midnight. Okay?"

"Yes. Thank you."

She swished away. The strapper withdrew his strappings.

"Her name is Mrs. Rice," Nick said. "She's okay, but keep an eye on that goon."

Nick, whose nickname was Whitey, looked much older than his twenty-eight years. His long-winded account of his arrest for possession was very vague. He wasn't a liar, just cautious, and when talking about himself he would only discuss candidly those facts that were a matter of record. (I could have been an informer.)

Around seven P.M., Mrs. Rice pushed in a small metal table with wheels on it and started passing out thermometers. When she handed me one, I stuck it in my mouth. The other patients started laughing.

"Robert," Mrs. Rice said, smiling, "that's a rectal thermometer. Let me put some more vaseline on it."

I surrendered it to her. "I was wondering why it had grease on it."

She smiled again and shook her head. "Now you know."

My temperature was normal. Mrs. Rice said that when I needed to go to the toilet, to go, but to come straight back to my bed. Nick took a bath. When he came back, he gave me a rundown on all of the patients in the ward. At nine o'clock the ward lights were dimmed and Nick retired. Slightly high, I slipped into a shallow nod. It had been a long day.

I was awakened by the screams of a terrified d.t.'s patient. Aside from my thumping heart, everything was still in focus, except that I had been strapped down one and one. My shallow nod must have had some depth because I could not recall being tied down. I wondered if my prediction as to when my habit should come down was right. The crying, pleading, begging wino was extremely unnerving. Gradually, the intensity of his cries for mercy subsided into soft sobs. . . .

25

It was a writhing orgasm! I tried desperately to conjure the dream that went along with that whopper, but was unsuccessful. I was on my back. It was morning. My attempt to throw back the sheet and slide out of bed was rudely checked by the forgotten harness. Was it summer or winter? There was a screen around my bed. The semen felt like ice water! I could see the pillow on Nick's bed. His head wasn't on it. Goose pimples. Damn, it was cold! Cold! Sound? I couldn't hear! I couldn't hear! Damn, it was hot! Hot! I couldn't breathe! Vomit! Vomit! Vomit. . . .

"Hold his head to the side! He'll choke!"

Shit! Vomit! Piss!

"Jesus Christ! He's doing everything at the same time!"

I could hear, but I couldn't see! Hot water! Hot! Hot! Hot! Nothing. . . .

A man was looking at me! Me? He cocked his head. He smiled . . . waved . . . smiled.

"Hey, go and get the nurse," he whispered. "I think he's coming around."

Nick. Nick's bed was empty! He was gone!

Swish. Mrs. Rice. *Swish, swish, swish.* . . .

She appeared from behind the screen, crossed her arms under her breasts and peered down at me. "Robert, if you can hear me, blink your eyes."

I blinked. Her radiant smile splashed all over me.

For eight days I had swerved precariously in, out and around the twilight zone. After my reentry on the ninth day, Mrs. Rice told me that Nick had been transferred to the V.A. hospital two days before.

"He refused to go, until I promised him that I would take special care of you. Did you know him before?"

"No," I answered, thinking, *funny, the beautiful people you meet in places like this.* . . .

26

Puppy Love!

Robert E. Chinn

Jay! God, how he loved Jay! Jay had been created just for him! The first time he saw Jay, he knew that they would become lovers, and the thought of making love to Jay had made him ache and sweat! He had never seen or known anyone like Jay. Jay really turned him on!

Was it the way Jay walked? Every step Jay took seemed to say: "Animal! Animal! Animal!" And Jay's walk made him feel like an animal—an animal in heat!

When he was introduced to Jay, he was glad that he was wearing sunglasses and they hadn't shook hands: if his eyes didn't give him away, his trembling hand surely would have! But he knew that Jay knew. He knew because when Jay was conversing with the man who had introduced them, he could smell his own heat, and Jay had been close enough to smell it too!

He had never had a mature woman. In school he had cornered a willing twelve-year-old girl; before he could get close enough to stick it in, he ejaculated on her stomach. When he was fifteen, his silly, virgin, seventeen-year-old cousin had let him do it; while trying to force it in, he got a "haircut"! After that painful experience with his cousin, he had retired wholly to masturbation.

God, how he wanted Jay! They would be good together! With Jay, he would be the perfect lover—Jay's man!

Their first kiss was a kiss that fused them so close together that it brought forth their seed! A kiss that he could never forget . . . or would ever want to forget! A kiss that gave his being meaning—Jay belonged to him; he belonged to Jay!

Mark had just turned twenty-one. Today was the last day of an indeterminate sentence (five years) he had received for breaking and entry. (When he was sixteen, he broke into a school in his neighborhood and stole a TV set.) Because of his size (6 feet 1 inch tall, 220 lbs.), he was sentenced to Bordentown Reformatory. In Bordentown, three years ago, he had stabbed two inmates critically (the two inmates and three others had tried to gang him). The authorities didn't prosecute him. Instead, they sent him to the state prison; he would have to max out. Tomorrow morning he would be released from New Jersey State Prison, Rahway.

Where should he go, Mark thought, as he lay on his bunk. Should he go home and stay with his mother, one older brother and two younger sisters until he got on his feet? Should he look for his father and stay with him? Or should he go and stay with his married sister? He wished that he didn't have to turn to his family for help; he was bitter about the fact that his family had visited him only seven times in five years! But he had to go somewhere. Where?

What would he do? Mark wondered. He was a dropout and had never worked anywhere except as a porter in the kitchen at Bordentown, and later, after being transferred to the prison, as a tier runner.

He thought: "When I get settled, I'll look up some of the guys I met in prison. They'll put me into somethin'. And when I cop a piece of money, I'll deck out a hip place for Jay and me!"

Jay was twenty-six and a notorious fag. Jay couldn't remember when members of his own sex didn't excite him. Jay was serving two to three years for slashing the face of another fag. His max would be up in six months. Jay was in no hurry to go anywhere. He was where his seat could and would get plenty of meat!

Jay's father was an ex-con. When Jay was a small boy, he used to look forward to visiting his father in prison. Jay's father had died in prison.

Jay was a jailhouse queen. He was sought after, propositioned, fought over, loved, and envied—Jay was the finest thing in the prison! And he knew it. He knew, also, that it was just a matter of time before he seduced that cute young boy who arrived in last week's shipment from Trenton: he was eighteen, yallar, well-built, with an afro that was groomed the same as Jay's —he was young, dumb and full of come! Jay wondered to what extent he would be able to corrupt his future plaything.

Jay smiled as he thought about all the young boys and men who had gasped his name before, during and after their crises! Most of them he had had his way with by making them perform for and on him the same acts that he had performed for and on them!

Jay's current plaything, Mark, would check out tomorrow morning. He was glad that Mark was leaving: he was beginning to tire of him. Jay had planned what role Mark would play under Mark's bunk during the yard period that afternoon. If Mark really loved him, Mark could make their parting a memorable occasion by assuming the passive role!

29

When the prison's P.A. system blared "yard out! all wings, yard out!" Mark's pulse began to quicken! Soon Jay would be in his arms! Soon his tongue would probe into Jay's sweet mouth! Soon he would prove his love for Jay by not placing a towel between them when he mounted: as Jay laid on his back, Mark would let Jay's bare member press against his stomach. Soon his nostrils would savor the pungent odors of their union!

Jay sneaked into Mark's cell and crawled under the bunk onto a soft, quilted pallet: Jay's pallet. A pallet that, like Jay, had absorbed the violences, the tears, the sweat, the frustrations, the humiliations, the jubilations and ejaculations that were ground into and onto it by Jay's countless lovers.

Jay's swift movements into the cell and under the bunk had startled Mark. He had been lost in thought, reflecting about what his homie had just told him: on the way back from the messhall this morning, his homie had seen Jay slipping a note to some new, light-skinned guy. "Aw, it was nothin'," Mark said to himself as he checked to make sure that no one could see under the blankets he had draped over his bunk. He then took off his shirt and pants, and crawled into their love nest!

The thought and danger of deflowering the trembling buttocks of a tender, but powerful, young boy could excite Jay and cause him to raise an erection that would be rigid enough to perform the act. During penetration, Jay would lose control of himself and come! As he came, he would plunge his vomiting meat to the hilt—then hold on for dear life! Afterwards, he would soothe his "bitch's" bleeding anus, orally! Jay was indeed a vile creature.

About ten A.M. the next morning, Mrs. Emma Mae Pools and her oldest son left the prison's administration building, stunned! Her son, Mark, wasn't coming home today . . . or ever! The superintendent had said that yesterday evening, during the inmates' recreation period, the wing officer had found Mark in his cell hanging from the light fixture. The officer had opened the door, cut Mark down, laid him on the bunk, then called the center and hospital for assistance. When the officer returned, he noticed a hand on the cell floor sticking out from under a blanket that was draped over the bunk. He looked under the bunk and found an unconscious inmate. Her son and the other inmate were pronounced dead on arrival at the prison's hospital. It appears that her son had strangled the other inmate to death, then committed suicide.

The superintendent gave them his condolences and a small manila envelope containing Mark's personal belongings.

As her son drove them back home, Mrs. Pools opened the envelope and withdrew what appeared to be a recent photograph of Mark in the prison's yard . . . with his arms wrapped around the slim waist of a very attractive woman . . . wearing hot pants. . . .

FRANK WILLIAMS

Rahway State Prison, Rahway, N.J.

Frank's main thing is poetry, for real, and he has the knack of saying the things he wants to say in the manner in which he wants to say them. He is serving sixty years, and for ten of those his entire world was relegated to the confines of four walls. Two years ago he stuck his head outside and consequently became enamored of a beautiful young woman named Suzanne, who returned his affection. At this juncture life has become quite miserable for both of them, because Frank wouldn't win any prizes for good behavior. Yet, in spite of the obstacles in front of them, the love affair continues to grow, and who knows—there's a lot of power in love.

A Home Is Not a House

Frank Williams

The night was one of contagious serenity, holding an omnipresent air of invocation, which seeped through the open pores of his skin, soothing him with its tranquillity. The many horrors of his life, locked inside of his head for so long, were now stripped of their confusing ability to destroy.

Chooky Johnson fished a crushed pack of cigarettes from his shirt pocket. After lighting one, he relaxed on the trunk of a fallen tree, his head tilted toward the sky, savoring the strong taste of tobacco. He blew a long shaft of smoke into the dancing flame of the match, until the flicking life was snuffed back into darkness.

In the background he heard an owl's *hoo*ing solo; then a frog along the edge of the lake struck a discordant note. Freeing his mind, he let his spirit rush away to become one with the surroundings, melting into the soft murmurs of the night.

Fireflies everywhere turned on their dancing lights, appearing like startled eyes suspended in the eternal veil of night. The earth's mighty heart moved beneath him, throbbing in time to the beat of his own awe-stricken ticker. Together he and the world became one, a single proliferation of continuity in existence. He was in a state of breathless rapture.

As he surveyed the calm surface of the lake, an indescribable sensation came alive in his body. *Beautiful* was the only epithet he could sheepishly offer, much aware of the insufficiency in empty-sounding words. He felt that his present awareness gave beauty to his existence and that his mind alone was the origin of it.

He took a final long pull on his cigarette and let the smoke ooze slowly out, before flipping the butt into the lake. He raised his head, shifting his position on the tree trunk. A shaft of moonlight struck him in the face, spotlighting the vestige of a million years of trial and tribulation. His features were long, lean, hard, covered with deep black hollows and planes, akin to the chiseled sharpness of a bronze statue. The backs of his hands were white, from burns received in early childhood. The palms were sterner, matching the coal-black complexion of his face, except for the tender neck skin between his jaw and Adam's apple, which had also been burned by the flames. In spite of marring scars, a keen sensitivity emanated from his young-old face, a kind of beauty in itself.

In silence, he studied the sky, deeply moved by the same impressive inspiration that had impelled men down through the ages to make gods of the heavenly bodies. He was unable to identify the star groupings, but at that moment he felt they held as much mystery and magic as ever before to anyone in the past.

"O, God," he sighed softly. "What is it with my life? Am I some kinda black Job, 'cause man, my burdens get heavier by the day."

Until that moment he had never given much thought to a god and even then he quickly reprimanded himself, passing the thought off as a momentary weakness.

Yet there remained a persistent awareness in the back of his mind that refused to completely annihilate the thought, mainly because of the warm and vague feeling of assurance it gave him.

He let his eyes travel the length of the small patch of water, to the boathouse, which squatted precariously over the water, beneath a cluster of night shadows. He absorbed the thin outline of the building into his train of thought, as it traveled backwards into a world ago.

On Sunday afternoons his father used to bring him here to fish. There was something mysteriously involved in life then, to the point of making him leery of sleep, as if he would miss the opportunity of experiencing some new and daring adventure, something that might not ever come his way again.

He was loved then. It wasn't the kind of love people talked about, no flags were waved high in the air attesting to the fact, but smiling eyes and tender actions shouted it out and he lived in a world of beautiful impressions. Love was in evidence, even when his father or mother became angry with him, which oftentimes resulted in getting his butt paddled. But who cared about any ol butt-whopping when one could really believe that the giver was hurt as much by them as the recipient.

Once he had gotten a fishhook caught in his finger and the tender agony that engulfed his father's face while he was removing the hook told a story that even a Shakespeare would have difficulty capturing with words. It was a tale of how pain could be transferred to another body through the medium of love.

Whenever they returned home from one of these jaunts, he would bubble out the afternoon's adventures and his mother would listen so attentively that he was certain the things he did were the most important happenings in her life.

37

But the drama of life is far different than those portrayed on a movie screen or jotted down on the pages of a novel, and every day there is a different song that underscores the realness of living. Sometimes it is a melody in bliss, while at other times the tune is one of pain and sadness. There is a certain intuitive force in youth that allows one to bypass the academic lack, and it was this innocent wisdom that warned Chooky of the plight in his parents' relationship. He "knew," in spite of a sudden showering of gifts, that the dregs of a dying love, a despairing love, were turning his parents against each other with all the cynicism of lost attraction.

His father was by nature a gentle and humble man, gentle almost to the extent of possessing some feminine characteristics. This gave him a great capacity for making friends, an outstanding ability for displaying tenderness with which he could establish easy relationships with both sexes. He possessed a great love for jazz and African poetry which in the aesthetic sense fostered the feminine traits within him. He liked to call himself ultraradical, embracing his views with the strength and conviction of a fire-and-brimstone preacher.

Chooky's father never had been aggressive in his role as parent and husband, and he somehow always made it a point to remain in the shadows of family activities. Earlier he provided well for his family, almost an insipid serf to the wheels of labor, and this alone throughout the years stood as his greatest accomplishment. Later he didn't even provide any support—the drugs took everything.

His mother was the exact opposite, a gregarious woman, gay and outgoing, always prepared to shower her social charms on anyone that happened to be in her company. She loved parties, the wild night life and flirting at every opportunity, usually with married men. She was viewed as the life of any party and quickly earned the reputation around the neighborhood as "the lover of married men" and "the dread of married women." This stigma Chooky loathed with a passion, and he failed to understand why his mother was partial to married men as partners in her illicit affairs.

Thoughts of his mother set off a chain of ancient tucked-away fantasies within Chooky, after his parents' terrible descent back to earth. They now regarded each other with the utmost distaste. His father's favorite phrase in regard to his wife was, "da dumbest bitch I had da misfortune to meet." Her inevitable reply was in reference to a "frustrated homo."

"That's etiquette, you ghetto-minded who'e," Chooky's dad would answer. "Education, which is something you don't know shit about."

"I ain't met a trick yet that was interested in whether or not I had a Ph and D certificate," Chooky's mother would shoot back.

"You dumb bitch! That's what's the matter now, you and niggers like you are the downfall of da whole race, and as long as niggers continue burying themselves in their own ignorance, da white man gonna keep a foot in y'all's ass. A good fuck is your total value!"

With a masochistic urge, Chooky's mind boarded the time machine again, to his first encounter with the word *whore,* though at the time its full meaning was not known to him. He first heard it used during the earlier years of his life, when things were not yet totally sour at home. His father, only when angry, made reference to his mother with that term. Chooky could tell, though, by the manner in which his father spewed out the phrase, that the meaning definitely was not an endearing one. As a matter of fact, he made it sound like the dirtiest thing the imagination could produce.

Soon after that home became an arena of arguments and fistfights. There was very little discretion employed and as a result, the other kids found fuel with which they could tease him relentlessly. The jibes about his parents, filthy-mouthed fights eventually approached the point of unbearable pain for Chooky. To top it off, he experienced some of his worst beatings in life during the course of these mad free-for-alls. That, coupled with the harassment of the neighborhood young bloods, caused Chooky to begin a retreat from the universe. He spent most of his time alone, trying to build a wall against the world's abuse.

He never could forget the time Linda Williams got up in front of his whole class and asked the teacher, Mrs. Belina, the meaning of the word "who'e."

Startled, Mrs. Belina stalled with a *why* in order to formulate an answer.

" 'Cause that's what my mama says Chooky's mother is."

The teacher's face burned suddenly red. "Don't you ever repeat that word again in this classroom!" she snapped, livid with rage. "Do you hear?"

The rest of the students had grown unnaturally quiet and a hushed silence hovered as Mrs. Belina shot a cold look around the room. Her glance hesitated at Chooky and he felt that by the softening of her tight features, she wished somehow there was some way to ease the hurt he was experiencing. But there was nothing to say. The damage was done and she remained silent, occasionally giving him one of those typical, sympathetic "white folks" looks over the rim of her glasses.

Shortly she sat down and opened a book on her desk. "Open your readers to page two-twenty-five," she said, overly briskly, "and when you are finished with that chapter, I will ask you questions about what you have read." She then turned her attention to marking some spelling tests that had been given the previous day.

Chooky stared at his reader, but the written pages held no meaning for him, only the hissing snickers and whispered remarks, always followed by a burst of subdued giggles. Each time he looked up, heads suddenly disappeared behind books. After a while he closed his own book and just sat there, staring blankly out a window. Mrs. Belina glanced up once, but said nothing.

The next time the laughter came, Chooky swung around and met the level gaze of Cleo Hill, the classroom bully. "Yo' mama is a who'e, . . . Yo' mama is a who'e," Cleo almost sang.

"Yo' mama is a double who'e!" Chooky shouted suddenly, stirring the whole room.

Cleo sprang from his desk, but the minute he made his move in the direction of Chooky, the teacher's screaming voice exploded like a thunder crack. "Stop! I tell you right now, we'll have none of that in my class! Do you hear?"

The class had erupted into a buzz of activity, students half out of their seats in eager anticipation of a rumble. "Get 'em, Cleo" or "Get 'em, Chooky" were the cries of encouragement, depending upon whom they liked the most. All this was stilled as Mrs. Belina walked down the aisle toward Chooky. She stopped in front of his desk and stood there, visibly having difficulty with her own self-control. Then she spoke.

"Go up to my desk and wait there."

Chooky slipped from his seat and did as he was told. He soon heard her talking to Cleo and when the bully piled out of his seat, Chooky guessed that she had told him the same thing.

"All right," Mrs. Belina began, when they were both in front of her desk, "what started this?"

Neither one of them said anything.

Her voice grew brittle. "I said, what started this?"

Cleo began talking, while Chooky stood silent, listening to the altered version. He didn't make any attempt

41

to defend himself, too ashamed to relate the truth. After Cleo was through, Mrs. Belina glared at him, surprised that a boy his age had acquired the ability to lie so glibly.

"You'll both stay after school," she said sharply, using her finger for emphasis. "Cleo, you go to that corner and stand there with your face to the wall. Chooky, you go to the other."

The remainder of the afternoon passed uneventfully, though the weighted silence of the other students told a tale of hostility and apprehension, until the recess bell splintered the quiet. Mrs. Belina kept Cleo and Chooky for a half hour, regarding both of their backs from time to time. Finally she shuffled the papers on her desk into order, then told the two they could go, Cleo first. On his way out the door he fixed Chooky with an unmistakable challenge in his eyes. Chooky returned it with equal intensity. Mrs. Belina motioned Chooky to the desk. He stood quiet, impatiently, while she labored uncomfortably over the same pile of papers. At length she spoke in a reasoning tone of voice.

"Do you think your mother would be proud of the way you carried on today? Gentlemen don't settle their differences in a violent manner. I'm sure your mother wants you to be a gentleman. Don't you think so?"

"Yes," Chooky replied softly, anxious to leave.

Mrs. Belina fumbled with the papers again. When she looked up this time, there was no mistaking the hint of irony that had invaded her eyes.

"Oh, you may go."

The second he stepped through the schoolyard door he noted the crowd of his classmates, gathered on the far side of the baseball field. He walked through the gate, away from them.

"There he is!"

He had covered less than half a block before he found himself surrounded, backed up against a storefront. A tight circle formed around him. Cleo stepped to the front and just stood there a moment, eyeing him up and down with contempt.

"Yo' mama's a whoe!" he spat finally. "Now whatcha gonna do 'bout that, big mouth?"

Chooky's answer came right away. To this day all he could recollect was a vague showering of Cleo with a volley of nonstop lefts and rights. The first blow was thrown impulsively, but the following was a flurry motivated by the combination of hate and his fear of the larger Cleo.

Cleo only managed to swing back once or twice, but these were ineffective against Chooky's frightened barrage, and he was no match for the smaller boy's fury. In short time Cleo went down, beaten into total submission.

When it was over, everyone stood with mouths hanging loose, eyes bulging in disbelief. Chooky felt an ache begin deep within him, because somehow he came to realize that he was far from the victor and that this was only the beginning of a lifelong struggle. A few months later he was expelled from school for continuously fighting with other students.

Almost before the last memory faded, another floated into his head and his body tightened at the first disgusting thought. He was fourteen and in his own mind's eye he saw himself climbing the stairs of his apartment building. At the top of the landing he froze, as a white sailor backed out of the rear apartment door, which swung open from his mother's bedroom.

He uttered not a word, only stood there in the subdued shadows of the staircase, listening and watching.

"See you again, baby," his mother patronized, kissing the sailor hard on the lips.

"I only have four days left on my leave, but I'll sure try to see you before I report back."

Chooky's mother stepped close. "Make it soon,

won't you, sugar?" She reached down and rubbed her hand up and down the front of his pants.

The sailor came away grinning, the afterglow of sated passion fresh in his mind. The smile disappeared at the sight of Chooky standing on the top step. That was something Chooky would never forget—fear in a white man's eyes. No, he would never forget that as long as he lived.

The sailor approached him hesitantly, a taut expression covering his paled face. When he was close enough to see that Chooky was only a young boy, his fear left, but there remained a hint of nervousness in the grin he tried and failed to produce. He fled quickly down the stairs.

Chooky gripped the apartment door firmly, turned the knob slowly, stepped only partially inside and looked around the interior. He no longer knew the place, it was alien, as if in all these years he was suddenly seeing it for the first time. Once the happy ring of laughter echoed off the walls. Once those same walls enclosed love and truth and warmth, providing security and safety for the essence of his complete being. The house had been a nest, a mellow cranny carved in the mountain of life by the industrious tenderness of sensitive hearts. No longer was it any of those. No longer was it a home. It was a house of hate! It was a house of lies and deceit! It was a house of ghastly silence! It was a boxing arena! It was a whorehouse! The only thing that lived there now was a roomful of exhausted dreams.

Chooky came back to the present, landing hard on reality's runway, stepping bitterly into himself again. No longer did the night fascinate him and the flickering evening eyes were only lightning bugs and the stars simply distant planets that meant nothing to him. Even the log he sat on had grown uncomfortable and the rough bark dug painfully into his rump.

"Where has it all gone?" he asked himself quietly, standing up and brushing off his clothes.

"Nowhere," his heart answered, "no-fucking-where at all!"

JOSEPH McCRORY

Rahway State Prison, Rahway, New Jersey

There isn't much one could write about Joe that's bad. He is a tall man, good-looking, soft spoken, and somehow manages to be liked and respected by everybody, without a whole lot of flag-waving. He is extremely intelligent and had no trouble breezing through a liberal arts course that was being given here at the prison. Writing isn't Joe's bag, but after reading some of the things he offhandedly jotted down, one sort of wishes he would take it up seriously.

Lasciate Ogni Speranza Voi Ch'Entrate
(Abandon all hope,
ye who enter these portals)

Prison life styles have changed considerably since the golden days of Cagney and Bogart. New heroes, such as Tiny Tim and the hirsute utopians like Snoopy, and various other anthropophagites have replaced the snarling monosyllabic giants of yesteryear. The lockstep has entered the Smithsonian and, when mentioned, is understandably mistaken for a variation of the Funky Broadway. If found in such a milieu, a revived Dillinger would, in a fit of outrage, immediately drill his resuscitator.

Of course, cultural diffusion from beyond the walls contributes highly to this phenomenon, as after all it is the age of the antihero. However, cultural lag from within, spiced with confused penal reform, is the real culprit. The result is a highly befuddled, bewitched and bewildered con, as opposed to the con of old, who knew who and what he was. This current distorted self-image, and the ensuing frustration, could in future years wreak more havoc than a score of Baby Face Nelsons raiding an FBI convention in search of revenge.

Some areas within the microcosm have seen little cultural lag, as tranquilizers have replaced clubs, but the results remain the same, and in most other areas confused administrative misoneists, who reached their level of incompetence the day they donned a badge, are still in command, and their schizoid natures are reflected in today's con.

Rare is the bird, *avis penitentiaria,* who conveys a message via the grapevine, as the ear of the administration is much more expedient, if not ingratiating. No longer is it in vogue, either, to refer to captors as hacks. Rather it has cachet to identify with them (pity). To top things off, the caged denizens are now referred to as "residents," and if that isn't enough, stripes have been phased out, too, and along with them the old "honor" among the loyal opposition. Should a freight train crash through the hallowed walls, residents would rush with alacrity to repair the breach—no wonder poor old Willie Sutton decided to throw in the towel. Gone, too, the way of the stripes, is the Friday-night flickering of the lights, when pals were consigned via electron to that blissful Valhalla of intrepid heroes, where Ma Barker, Cockeyed Dunn, The West Side Mob, The Purple Gang and yes, even old Jesse, were on hand to meet them.

Alack and alas, now the venerated pantheon lies in ruin, desecrated by administrative iconoclasts and stultified traitors. The wretched con, stripped of gods and goal, is demoralized and puzzled no end. Visions of expiring in a prison hospital ward, surrounded by fellow geriatric robots, torment his mind and weaken his will. Thus he accepts the proffered Lethean cup and consequently descends to anomie. Perhaps this effect is what society desires, but the point is moot. Yet the impact on personality disintegration justifies exploration, if for no other reason than because it's there.

However, in those wee small hours, when the whistling wind playing on the bars is counterpointed by the sweet dirge of the hack's crescendoing keys, when scenes from *High Sierra* or *Twenty Thousand Years in Sing Sing* are roaring through my mind, I will open a can of beans and toast the vanished giants of days long gone. And sometimes, when the moon is right, I'll hear the ghost of Duke Mantee say, with that endearing snarl, "What's a nice con like you doing in a place like this?"

Save a towel for me, Willie—I've had it!

DARYL SMITH

New Mexico State Penitentiary, Santa Fe, New Mexico

Little Brother Mad

Daryl Smith

The match flared in the darkness as I lit my fourth
cigarette in half an hour. I glanced at my watch before
I shook the match out. It was after eleven-thirty, but
it seemed like hours since I'd parked the car here to
wait for the other three to come out of the liquor store.

I had never violated the law before, but they made
it sound so easy and here I was, parked in a dark
alley in my brother's car, waiting for a signal to pull
up behind the liquor store that was being burglarized.
My nerves tingled with excitement as my eyes stayed
glued to the darkness ahead—the direction from which
the signal would come. I puffed on my cigarette and
from the light of its fiery tip, checked my watch again.
Eleven-fifty. Time sure was dragging.

A sharp whistle broke the stillness. I flipped the
cigarette out the window and cranked the car up, feeling all thumbs as I fumbled with the gearshift. With
the headlights out, I drove down the alley and braked
to a stop at the rear door of the liquor store.

"Kill the engine and give me the keys!" my brother
Joseph hissed.

I did as I was told. The rear door opened and the

back seat and floor were quickly stacked up with cases of liquor. The trunk was opened and that, too, engulfed case upon case of stolen whiskey.

Joseph came around to the driver's side. "Move over," he told me. "I'll drive."

The trunk slammed closed and the other two climbed in, one in front with me and Joe, the other in the back with the cases of hot liquor.

"Let's go!" someone whispered.

Joe drove the car out of the alley and onto a dimly lit street. After the car gained some speed he flipped on the headlights. The car was a tomb of silence and no one said anything. If they were like me, their hearts were thumping too hard for any talking.

I felt proud of my big brother though. I knew it was wrong to steal, but still I admired his proficiency, his nerve. It was obvious he didn't feel the same fear I felt. Of course, he was four years older than me and this wasn't his first experience with crime. Maybe that made a difference. Maybe I wouldn't be so scared the next time, and I knew there would be a next time.

Joe broke the ring of silence. "Bust open one of those cases and let's have a drink."

I heard the tearing of cardboard and clinking of bottles in the back. "Hope you guys like scotch," the guy in the rear said. "That's what I opened."

"Scotch is okay," Joe said.

The bottle made the rounds. I didn't really want to drink, but I didn't want to seem like a know-nothing kid either, so when the bottle came to me I drank. The brown liquid screamed down my throat like an avalanche of hot lava. I gasped.

Joe grinned. "Take it easy, little brother. That stuff's not water."

The little exchange between me and Joe seemed to ease the tension, and it was as if a gray cloud had

56

suddenly been lifted from the car. There was no visible difference, but it was something you could feel.

"Is the fence expecting this stuff tonight?" the guy next to me asked.

"Yeah," Joe said. "He said he'd have the cash on hand. I'm going to drop my little brother off at home first."

I didn't want to go home, but I didn't want my parents to become suspicious either. They were good parents and tried to give Joe and me the things we needed. If they knew we were out stealing, it would be an injury they would never recover from. I didn't want them to ever find out. Half a block from our two-story brick house Joe stopped the car and I climbed over him.

"If they ask where I went," Joe said, "tell them I had to take my date home."

"Okay," I replied.

"And don't get too close to them, or they'll smell the scotch on your breath."

I nodded and stood there a moment watching the auto move out of sight. We had told our parents we were going to a drive-in movie. I didn't enjoy lying to them, but there wasn't much else I could do.

Walking the half block toward home, I kicked a rock along in front of me. I didn't feel guilty about stealing the liquor and, in fact, felt a sense of calmness, a sudden tallness.

My mother was sitting in the living room reading a magazine when I walked quietly in the door. My father must have gone to bed because the next day was Monday and a working day for him.

"Where's Joe?" my mother asked with a smile. "I didn't hear the car drive up."

"He let me off at the corner," I said. "He had to take his date home."

"Oh, well, you better get to bed. You've got school tomorrow."

"Okay, Mom, good night."

Joe and I had separate bedrooms on the second floor of the house and I climbed the stairs to mine, unbuttoning my shirt as I went. I didn't know how long it would be before Joe came home, but I planned to wait up. I wasn't tired and my nerves were still pretty active, but in a strange, quiet sort of way. I undressed and lay on my bed. About an hour later I finally heard Joe coming up the stairs. I went to meet him.

"Everything went all right," he said, pulling a wad of bills out of his pocket. He peeled off two and handed them to me. "I'd give you more, but I'm afraid you might get careless and flash it. Anytime you want some more, just let me know. Now go to bed. I'll see you in the morning."

"Okay," I told him.

I went back to my room and put the bills in the pocket of the pants I planned on wearing to school. I never bothered to look at how much money Joe gave me, and I didn't really care. Mother and Father gave me money for school every day and I always managed to save a little for anything else I might need. I had a difficult time getting to sleep. It was the big night of my life; I'd pulled off my first burglary and got away with it.

I awoke the next morning and thought immediately of the previous night's escapade. I rushed to the dresser mirror to examine myself. I looked the same, no taller, no broader, no more of a man than I'd been the day before. I dressed, brushed my teeth, washed my face, combed my hair, and went down to breakfast.

The meal was a quiet one. I sat across the table from Joe, every once in a while glancing at him over a spoonful of oatmeal. He never looked at me.

After breakfast Joe and my father left for the factory where they worked. I gathered up my books, pecked my mother on the cheek, and hurried off to school.

I didn't think much of school, with its clanging bells, mobs of rushing students, teachers with nothing on their minds but graduating their pupils. I planned to quit as soon as I was old enough.

When the dull morning classes were finally over, I hurried to the cafeteria, hoping to beat the long line of eaters. I filled my tray, pulled out one of the bills Joe gave me and went to the cash register. I was shocked to see Hamilton's face—Joe had given me two twenty-dollar bills! I paid for my lunch and quickly pocketed the change.

I didn't see much of my brother during the rest of the school year. He wasn't home much anymore and though my parents were concerned about him and his running around, they never scolded him. I didn't do much studying, but my grades in school stayed around average and I spent most of my time simply daydreaming. Countless times I rehashed in my mind the liquor store robbery, but Joe never took me along on any more of his jobs, though I knew he was involved in some.

When summer finally arrived, I looked forward with pleasure to the three months of pure relaxation and fun. By then Joe was associating with a wild bunch. He was drinking like a fish and spent a lot of money on his car. I knew he didn't make enough at the factory to buy booze every night and to also pay for the work on his car. Neither was he able to hide from our parents the things he was doing, nor did he try. Many nights I heard him stumbling up the stairs in a drunken daze.

In June he was arrested for drunken driving and lost his license, but that didn't slow him down. He got one of his wild friends to drive his car for him and his escapades continued.

I longed to share in his excitement, the fast life he was leading, but not once did he ask me to come along and I was greatly disappointed. My parents were glad though and didn't trust me with him; they'd lost all faith in him.

One warm July evening I was walking home from a movie when Joe's car pulled up to the curb next to me, the tires screaming in protest at the sudden braking. Two girls in the car giggled loudly.

"Hey, little brother!" Joe yelled. "Climb in! I want to talk to you."

I didn't know the guy who was driving or either of the girls. I got into the rear seat, where Joe sat with his arm around a buxom blonde. The car shot away from the curb with a surge that threw me back in the seat.

"Want a beer?" Joe asked. He had a can clenched between his knees and a case of the brew sat on the floor between his feet.

"I guess so," I replied, unsure of myself.

"Give my little brother a beer," Joe told the girl.

She obeyed, like a well-trained servant, pulling the can from the case and opening it. Her soft hand brushed mine as I reached for the beer. I blushed and she smiled.

"Thank you," I said, and a funny expression passed across her face.

"Hey, little brother," Joe said with a broad grin. "How'd you like to make fifty dollars?"

"Doing what?" I asked, not really caring. I was more than eager for a replay of the excitement I'd felt the night of the liquor store.

"Tell you about it later," Joe said and offered me a cigarette, which I declined. I'd been smoking since I was thirteen, but I didn't feel like one right then.

60

"Okay," I said and sipped my beer. I didn't like it. It tasted sour and bitter.

We rode around town for over an hour, drinking, with Joe kissing the blonde, nibbling on her neck and making her giggle. Three empty beer cans lay at my feet and my head felt light and dizzy.

Finally the guy behind the wheel pulled over in front of a drugstore and ordered the girls out. They protested, until Joe repeated the order, then climbed meekly out of the car.

"Drive," Joe told the guy behind the wheel, "and I'll tell my brother what's happening."

"You sure he can handle it?" the guy wanted to know. "He looks kind of young."

"He can handle it," Joe assured him.

"All right," the guy replied, and gunned the engine.

"Listen," Joe said, as we rode toward a destination unknown to me, "we're going to heist a gas station. Everything should go smooth enough. All you have to do is park around the corner and be ready to take off when we jump in."

"I can do that easy enough," I assured him.

He slapped me on the back. "I knew I could count on you."

"There's the place," the guy behind the wheel said. We rode past a large service station.

I looked it over quickly as we went past. It was a well-lit place and busy. The lone attendant had his hands full, trying to take care of four pumps. I was about to say something about the customers, but Joe beat me to it.

"One of us is going to have to catch the cars coming in."

"I'll wait on them," the guy said.

"Okay, park the car. Little brother, when we get out you jump behind the wheel. Keep the motor running

61

and be ready to move as soon as we get back. We shouldn't be more than five or ten minutes."

"I'll be ready," I promised.

The driver parked the car on a side street a half block from the service station. Joe opened the glove compartment and pulled out a blue revolver, its finish glistening in the dim light. He shoved the pistol in his waistband, under a thin jacket he was wearing, and climbed out. The other guy followed and I jumped into the driver's seat. I watched them in the rear-view mirror until they disappeared around a corner.

Once again the weird excitement was in my blood and getting stronger with each heartbeat. The light dizziness brought on by the beer subsided and I was cold sober and alert. My palms were sweating and I dug in my pocket for a cigarette and lit it.

I was still on my first smoke when three gunshots broke the evening air. The sharp cracks echoed through the city blocks and rumbled along the streets like a volley of cannons. I spun in the seat and stared out the rear window. Two more shots sounded and seemed to carry a heavier tone.

I fought the impulse to flee, but I couldn't leave my brother, no matter how frightened I became. The screaming of sirens grew audible in the distance and sweat started leaking from every pore in my body. My hands shook wildly. I kept looking out the back window, but there was no sign of Joe or his associate.

A police cruiser flew by, its red light flashing and the siren blaring. They paid no attention to me or the car. I kept watching for Joe, but I knew something had gone wrong, I knew he wasn't coming.

A few minutes later there was a prolonged volley of shots, then silence and I knew it was over. I laid my head on the steering wheel and cried. Somehow, I'd make them pay. I didn't know who or how, but somebody would pay for Joe's life. No longer was I experiencing the wild excitement, only cold hatred.

I wiped my eyes and started the car. I was going home; my parents would need their only son.

The police brought the tragic news to my parents that same night. Mother wept bitterly, but my father simply stood in the doorway, his face a mask of shocked bewilderment. While the policeman continued spouting out his sorrow, I fought down the urge to spit in his face. Finally I told the cop to go, pulled my father out of the doorway and sat him down. I didn't shed any tears. Joe didn't need tears.

My brother's funeral was a congregation of weeping, but I sat quietly clenching my teeth in anger. Later, as I walked past his coffin, I bent and kissed his cold forehead. "They'll pay, Joe," I whispered. "They'll pay."

The day after the funeral I told my parents that I wasn't going back to school. My mother tried to argue, but my father accepted my decision calmly. He hadn't said twenty words since Joe's death, though I think he knew I was with Joe that night. He saw me bring the car home.

Later, on the night after the funeral, I was in my room trying to form a plan of revenge. My father came in.

"Are you going to leave us?" he asked, sitting down on the edge of my bed.

"I haven't decided yet." I stared at my father. He seemed so old, an old stranger.

"If you decide to go, don't say anything to your mother; just go. If you need money, let me know. . . ."

"All right."

He took my hand and shook it. "Good luck, son," he said softly.

"Thank you, sir." I felt funny. It was the first time my father had shook my hand, and the last. . . .

Later that night he loaded his twenty-gauge shotgun, stuck the barrel in his mouth, and pulled the trigger with his toe. The blast blew out the top of his head, killing him instantly.

Two ambulances came, one for my father's body, one for my mother, who had gone into hysterics. After they left and the police finished with their little interrogation, I stood in the living room and stared at my father's blood and brains splattered all over the wall. I wanted to cry, but I couldn't; there were no tears left in my heart, only cold bitterness.

I went to my room and packed some clothes into an overnight bag. While I searched the house for some money, I found a .45 in the bottom drawer of my father's dresser. He'd brought it home from the war. I stuck it in my belt and started looking for the shells that went with it. I finally found them in the cabinet where he kept his shotgun. I put the bag, shells and the automatic in Joe's car and went to the garage. In the darkness I found the five-gallon can of gas we used for the lawnmower. I returned to the house and poured gasoline on my father's bed, on all of the downstairs furniture, on Joe's bed. I finished by drenching the wall where my father's brains were drying.

I found an old newspaper, wadded it up, lit it, and threw it on the wall. The gasoline ignited with a puff, turning into a fiery tongue that licked upward and grew larger with each passing second. I watched the blaze for a few minutes, glad I'd done what I'd had to do.

I ran from the house and climbed into Joe's car. I pulled out the .45 clip and put in some shells, then jammed it back into the gun and started the car. By the time I was out of the driveway the house was a blazing inferno and, like the roaring fire, I felt a fury building up inside of me, a fury that couldn't be held or restrained.

I stomped on the gas pedal and held it to the floor

64

all through town. I ran through red lights, stop signs and up one-way streets, feeling no fear. Death had no chain of terror on my heart or on my mind, and for me the word *death* was simply that—a word.

A siren wailed and a red light started blinking along behind me. The murderers of my brother, my father and, yes, my mother too, were looking for another victim. They didn't suspect that the hunted was hunting this time also.

My hand groped on the seat next to me for the .45 and when I found it, the butt felt cold against my palm. I slowed the car down and stopped on the side of the road. I hoped Joe knew somehow that I was going to get his vengeance for him.

I watched the murderer climb out of his red prowl car, citation book in hand, and walk toward the open window of Joe's car. I pulled back the slide of the automatic, forcing a shell into the chamber.

"Okay," the killer grumbled, "let's see your . . ."

His words stalled and his eyes bulged as he stared into the hungry barrel of the .45. I squeezed the trigger; the gun roared and jumped in my hand, and his face disintegrated. I watched his hat fly into the middle of the street and roll around into a little circle before flopping still.

I put the pistol in my lap and drove away, no longer feeling the urge to speed. I stopped at every light, obeyed every traffic sign. I was exhausted, tired—the rage had burned itself out.

I stopped at a motel near the edge of town and rented a room. I needed to sleep, a long peaceful sleep, before the murderers came. I'd have to be ready. I parked the car in front of the rented room and went inside, carrying the .45 and the shells with me. I flopped on the bed, not bothering to turn on the lights; I suddenly appreciated the darkness.

I felt the need to talk, but there was only one person

65

who could possibly understand me, so I talked to him. "They'll be coming soon, Joe," I mumbled, fingering the gun. "But you know how it is, right?

"Don't worry about Mom, Joe. They've got her in the hospital now, but I think she'll decide to come with us later."

A squad car screamed to a halt in front of the motel. I smashed the big show window and pulled off two shots in the direction of the car lights. The noise rolled along the parking lot with a dull rumble.

"Here they are, Joe." I fired again, giggling at the sound of tinkling glass and the dousing of a headlight.

Another cruiser slid behind the first. I jerked the trigger again, liking the feel of the big .45's recoil in my hand. I filled the clip again and slapped it home. Someone called my name over a bullhorn. It was loud.

"They're calling me, big brother. It's time to go. Don't worry, Joe, I evened things up for you."

I opened the door and stepped out. I couldn't see what to shoot at because of the spotlights shining in my eyes, but I fired in the direction of the voice that was calling my name.

Things started tearing at my body, feeling like a hot rainstorm. I fell to my knees and still the scorching rain continued. When it stopped raining, I was on my back, lying in a pool of my own warm blood. The night was quiet when a silver-gray blanket spread itself over me and I looked up into the smiling joker-face of Death.

"Think they'll say Joe's little brother was mad?" I asked Death.

He didn't answer. . . .

KATY MOORE

Minnesota Correctional Institution for Women,
Shakopee, Minnesota

What Price Sacrilege?

Katy Moore

Cut off my hands! I'm a thief! I did great sin against the God of America—Affluence! I stole money! Can you imagine a crime more horrendous? No petty rap for me, such as murder, rape or genocide. I had to go all the way and take the token of Worship right from the Temple. I walked into a bank and through trick and artifice, did willfully and maliciously swindle MONEY from the Sacred House of Commerce! I didn't even have the decency to carry a gun. I simply walked in, presented a worthless scrap of paper, and asked for Cash in exchange. I realize, of course, that had I used a weapon of some sort, society would have been more lenient; because the Gods Violence and Bloodshed are almost as dear to the hearts of America as Affluence . . . as apple pie. Fool that I was, I dared incur the wrath of a people devoted to their God, so much so that they would sacrifice anything for its protection.

Had I used a gun the Bankers, Priests and Priestesses would have felt much better, saying, "She did it honestly, from up front," but I didn't and they said instead, "She's astoundingly crafty and cunning, and simple folks are no match for this monster.

"What to do now? What must we do with this unholy despoiler of the Temple? Yes, of course, we'll lock the wretched woman away in a jail cell for a year or two, pending a "speedy" hearing, then, when we find her guilty, we'll send her to a nice reformatory where she can further ponder her sins and repent."

I'm touched, dear people! But I say, "NO!" Rather than lock me away, cut off my hands, my ears, brand my flesh as in days long past. It would be kinder than this lengthy surgery, which cuts out my heart, my soul and sears my brain.

Is there money enough to pay for a human soul? Can your affluence replace a broken spirit? Can you assess materially the emotional damage done by one day in jail—let alone 365 or 3650?

You must concur with these practices, because prison sentences are meted out by judges, some of your most affluent representatives, and carried out by law enforcement officers who couldn't find Appalachia or a slum district on their radar screens. These judicial practices only reflect the desires of the majority—you. As long as you stand silently by and support these archaic antiquities, my tears, my pain and eventually my blood, are on your hands!

ARTHUR L. DEVLIN

Massachusetts State Prison, Norfolk, Massachusetts

Art is the type of author and individual that one could sit down and write a novel about, without ever running out of fascinating ideas and accomplishments to relate. He has "been down" over twenty years, yet somehow never fails to perk someone up with his letters, poetry, essays and stories. Art is a writer's writer, and writes what he feels and knows. Simply by being himself he is capable of eliciting from a reader either a smile or a frown, a tear or a laugh, and after all, isn't that what writing is all about? More important, Art Devlin is a gentleman in a jungle and he hasn't let twenty years in prison stunt his growth. For his future he would like to walk free again and to have an agent handle his writing for him. If there was justice in the world, he would have had both a long time ago.

Fish

Arthur L. Devlin

When I look back at the way I acted during most of my four-year stretch in San Quentin Prison—class of 1952—I realize that in those days I was close to being a stone nut, as the saying goes. It's easy to rationalize, to point out that it was my first bit, that I wasn't con-wise, but the truth of the matter is simply that I was a prime candidate for the funny farm.

I was twenty-three years old when I walked through Quentin's main gate in February of 1948, carrying three consecutive five-years-to-life sentences on my back. I'd been the leader of a holdup gang that had knocked off thirty-one hotels and motels in and around Hollywood before the fuzz finally put an end to our spree. A first offender with a good army record behind me, I might have been given a break and had my sentences run concurrently, but instead of copping out along with the rest of my crime-partners, I'd demanded, and received, a jury trial. That had been my thirty-second mistake.

Quentin's physical setup has changed over the years, but when I hit the joint each new con—or "fish"— was held for approximately three months in the West

73

Block Section, known then as the "Guidance Center." Throughout the ninety-day period a fish wore castoff Army or Marine Corps green fatigue uniforms instead of the regular "Q" blues. He was given every kind of test ever devised, presumably to discover the workings of his criminal mind. Also, he remained under constant surveillance by a plethora of screws, counselor-psychologists and psychiatrists who seemed to accomplish little except to give him the feeling that everyone was staring at him, which they were.

I got off to an ingeniously devilish start in the Guidance Center by refusing to take the battery of tests. I think the resultant rumble registered on the seismograph at Palo Alto. None of the counselors had ever heard of such a thing. It just wasn't cricket! I told them I couldn't see what my intelligence, or lack of intelligence, had to do with my doing an easy bit, and I let it go at that. After all, I knew what the outside world thought of cons anyway. Hadn't I seen all those prison pictures where everyone doing time talked out of the sides of their mouths and all that jazz?

Just nineteen days after I entered "Q" I was up on Isolation, or "The Shelf" as it is better known, the punishment section on the top floor of the North Block, just opposite Death Row. I was put up there for throwing rocks, which doesn't sound so terrible. What made it bad was that I threw the rocks at a screw. He was sitting in a guard shack up on top of the South Block at the time. I'd just wanted to shake him up a little bit. He had a very irritating habit of running out of the shack at the least provocation and pointing his rifle down into the West Block exercise yard as we cons walked around. Once he busted a couple of caps just for laughs, and it was lucky that nobody got hit. My rock-throwing was a little hint for him to cool it. Instead I was the one to get cooled. I spent eleven days on The Shelf.

When my brainwashing period in the Guidance Center was over—they gave up trying to make me take the tests—I was transferred over to Quentin side one Saturday morning. A beefy screw led me up to my cell on the fourth tier of the South Block "A" Section and let me throw my belongings inside. Then I went back down the stairs and out into the Big Yard.

Back in 1948 there were over five thousand cons in "Q". The Big Yard, on the long weekends, was almost solidly packed with blue-clad figures. I felt conspicuous in my brand-new clothes and made the best of a bad moment by merging with the crowd, as if I knew where I was going and who I was looking for. After a few minutes I stopped playing the role and went over and sat down on one of the benches under the big shed and listened to the music coming from the loudspeakers hanging on the side of the North Block overlooking the yard.

A couple of hours later I felt like I was growing out of the bench. Just to break the monotony I turned to the con sitting beside me, a guy around forty years old. "Got the time?" I asked.

"Sure, kid," he said, winking at me lasciviously. "Got the place?"

Just my luck, I thought.

"What I mean is," I said, stupidly blundering on, "do you know what *time* it is?"

"Why?" he said, laughing now. "You goin' someplace?"

"I am now," I said, my face red as a beet as I jumped up and flew recklessly off into the wild blue yonder.

The screws cleared the yard at eleven-thirty. I tagged on to the end of one of the long lines filing into the South Block and made my way up to the fourth tier. A short, curly-haired con was standing in front of my cell.

"You must be my new cell partner," he said. "My name's Aubrey Philpott, but you can call me anything except late for breakfast."

"Okay," I said, glad that he had a sense of humor. "I'm Art Devlin."

A loud bell rang and the tier man hoisted the long iron bar blocking the tops of the cell dors. Aubrey opened the door and we stepped inside. I pulled the door shut behind me. After the screws went by for the count, we took turns washing up. Fifteen minutes later we were on our way to chow.

That night after supper, when we were locked in until seven-thirty the following morning, Aubrey filled me in on how it was on Quentin side, sparing none of the gory details. He worked in the jute mill, the place where I had been banished by the Guidance Center Classification Committee as punishment for my bad attitude. Aubrey told me his job in the mill was as a weaver on a loom. He added that maybe there were worse jobs in "Q", but offhand he couldn't think of any.

At one minute past eight o'clock on Monday morning I stood in front of a desk in the jute mill office, looking down at Mr. Stoy, who was affectionately known as "Little Caesar."

"Well, Devlin!" Stoy yelled at me. "I'm putting you to work on a loom! Mind your own business down here and do your work and we'll get along fine!" He opened a desk drawer and handed me a pair of small scissors. "These belong to you now. If you lose them it'll cost you the money to buy another pair, understand?"

I nodded.

"Okay! Get out there and report to Murphy! He'll show you where to go to work."

I turned and walked out of the office and in to the jute mill work area. It was bedlam. The noise was unbelievable. Cons were scurrying frantically back and forth around the looms like madmen, cursing, pounding the machines with their fists in frustration. The racket was almost unbearable, a mixture of machinery humming, the looms clacking, an occasional deep booming sound drowning everything else out momentarily.

"Everything look okay to you?" somebody bellowed in my ear.

I looked behind me. A big, husky screw was standing there, smiling at me.

"Wow!" I said, grinning back at him. "Those looms sure make a lot of noise, don't they?"

"Do you want we should put mufflers on them for you?" the screw said, still smiling.

I caught on. "You must be Murphy."

"*Mister* Murphy to you, bucko!" he roared.

"Oh, sorry! Mr. Stoy said I should report to you."

Murphy grabbed my pass and led me over to a big board that had a lot of identification cards inserted in the various slots all over the face of it. "Put your ID card in Slot Number 19!" he barked. "When you leave, pick it up! Go through the same routine every time you come in or go out of the jute mill. Got it?"

"Got it!" I said.

He moved over to a square box that was nailed to one of the wooden posts jutting up from the floor. He opened the box. "This is the scissors box. You put your scissors in the same numbered hole as your ID card. Number 19. If you forget to turn them in before you go out of the jute mill, it's a beef. Got it?"

"Got it!" I said.

Murphy couldn't make up his mind if I was a wise guy or not. "I'm putting you on a loom as a helper," he went on. "Your weaver'll show you what to do. Come with me!" He brought me over to loom Number 19. He yelled something to a big con who was standing

77

in front of the machine watching the cloth, then Murphy cut out.

I waited at the back of the loom until the big con finally walked around to me.

"My name's Eddie!" he shouted. It was the only way to be heard above the appalling racket. "I'm your weaver. Ever work on a loom before?"

"No!" I screamed at the top of my lungs. "I never even saw one of these contraptions until a few minutes ago!"

Eddie shuddered. "Well, I suppose we got to start someplace." Then he reached down and took my right hand in his and said, "You know how to hold the scissors?"

I felt like an idiot with him holding my hand. He must take me either for a fag or a moron, I thought. Or both.

"Sure!" I shrieked, freeing my hand from his and working the scissors in the usual way, as if to cut out paper dolls.

"That ain't the way I mean!" Eddie yelled. He grabbed my scissors and placed them flat on my palm. "Stick your little finger through the hole in the handle nearest it!" When I did, he said, "Now you got it!" and moved the tips of the blades with only my forefinger and thumb.

It felt weird and uncomfortable to me. "That's a crazy way to hold a pair of scissors!" I shouted.

A look of disgust came over his face. "Listen, kid! They been holding scissors like that ever since they invented the loom. It makes it easier to clear the strings and tie knots, so dummy up and learn how! I ain't got all day to fuck around with you! I got cloth to put out!"

I shut up and began to learn my job. The helper's part was to pick the strings clean of fuzz, and to make certain none of the knots got hung up in any of a series of eyelets through which the strings ran on out to the front of the loom. The big, spool-like thing that fed the strings through the eyelets was called a "warp," and it held 512 strings in all. From time to time I would spy an extra large knot and then cut out the bad section of string and replace it with a good piece from a bunch that was hung up on the back of the loom. Eddie showed me the "weaver's knot," and I was just beginning to learn how to tie it real fast when the whistle blew for dinner.

After chow in the Big Mess Hall, and a half-hour break in the yard, I went back to the mill.

"I'm on what they call 'task,'" Eddie told me. "I got to make seventy-three yards of cloth a day, so that means the loom's got to keep going all the time, understand?" He led me around to the front of the loom for the first time and showed me how to stop and start the loom by means of a lever that stuck up from the surface on the right-hand side. He changed shuttles for me a couple of times, just to let me see how it was done.

"That doesn't look too difficult," I said.

"It ain't, once you catch on. Just remember that we ain't making no rag if the machine's stopped. The key to putting out seventy-three yards a day is to keep the loom going."

"Keep the loom going," I repeated.

"Right!"

I returned to my station at the back of the loom and managed to keep the strings clean without too much trouble. It got so easy after a while that I began to daydream. Some time later I suddenly became aware of a slight change in the noise level, and when I looked up I noticed that the loom had stopped. Without a second thought I raced around to the front and hit the lever, determined to keep putting out that cloth. Too late I noticed that Eddie was kneeling down at the left-hand side of the loom, with his head stuck into the undersection where the gears were. When the loom clacked into action he gave a loud bellow and jerked back out of the way just in time.

"Dammit!" he yelled. "What the hell's wrong with you?"

"Nothing," I said, feeling like a fool. "But you told me to keep the loom going all the time, didn't you?"

"Not when I got my head stickin' into it, you creep!"

"Oh!" I said.

He glared at me. "Get around to the back where you belong, and let me take care of the front from now on. Got it?"

"Got it!" I said.

After that first hectic day in the jute mill I brought some cotton to work with me. I stuffed it deep into my ears to shut out most of the noise. The other cons kept looking over at me like I was a ding-a-ling, which is Q-talk for a nutcake.

At around nine-thirty on my first Thursday morning in the mill, I was busy working when I heard a whistle blow. The cons in my section shut off their looms, and everybody made a mad dash for the ID card rack. Eddie cut out along with the rest of them, without a word to me. I wondered what the hell was going on. I walked over to Mr. Murphy and asked him where they had all gone.

"Shower day!" he shouted. "You've got thirty minutes to get on over to the laundry building, grab a shower, and get back here to work!"

I put my scissors in the box, picked up my ID card, and strolled out the rear gate of the jute mill to the laundry building, which was located next to the mill. When I turned the corner I saw at least sixty cons standing around, sweating out the line, which was moving very slowly. By the time I made it inside the building and up to the clothing window, my half-hour was almost up. I handed my ID card to one of the queens who made up the laundry crew.

"Say, you're cute!" the queen said softly, his fingers brushing my hand as he took my ID card. He swished away from the window and came right back with my clean clothing issue. He rolled his eyes at me. "How long have you been in Quentin, honey?"

"Not that long," I said. I took my clothes and fought my way to an empty spot on one of the benches over against the far wall. I stripped, and it took me ten more minutes before I managed to spy a jet of water that wasn't being used. The shower setup was a community-type thing, either by necessity or choice, I wasn't sure which. Not at first. Then so many guys began to rub asses with me and give me little nudges here and there that I finally got suspicious and decided enough was enough. I rinsed off and squirmed back through the wet, naked bodies to the bench. I got dressed, turned in my dirty clothes, got another sexy look from the queen, and walked back to the mill.

Murphy was waiting for me at the scissors box. "Oh, hello!" he said, feigning surprise. "I thought maybe you'd drowned over there."

I smiled at him. "Nice of you to worry."

"I wasn't worrying, wise guy. Just hoping." He glanced down at his wristwatch. "You've been gone almost an hour," he said. "Let's you and me go in and see Mr. Stoy!"

"I've already seen him," I said.

Murphy grabbed my arm. "Not on a beef, you ain't!"

Mr. Stoy leaned back in his swivel chair, studying my folder and making a little humming noise. After a few moments he peeked up over the top of his glasses at me. "What took you so long to shower, Devlin?"

"I had to wait until I got under some water," I said. "It works better that way."

Mr. Stoy pursed his lips and glanced at Mr. Murphy

81

before his eyes swung slowly back to me. "I see. You're a comedian, eh?"

His coolness flustered me. "I'm no comedian," I said.

He adjusted his glasses. "True enough. Now that we have that settled, let me inform you that I'm fining you one dollar. If you're not back within the specified time next Thursday, it will cost you another dollar."

I laughed. "I haven't been here long enough to earn any money, yet. How can I pay the fine?"

He was ready for that one. "Well, it looks as though you're going to be with us for quite a while, with your attitude, so we won't worry about the money. We'll just take it out of your future earnings." He closed my folder. "Now go back to your machine!"

"Yes, master!" I said, wheeling about and heading for the door. My hand had just touched the knob when Mr. Stoy's voice stopped me.

"Devlin!"

I turned.

"You can't win, Devlin."

I shrugged. "I can die trying."

"Yes," he said. "You probably will."

The strange thing about it is that, in a way, he was right.

The Chair

Arthur L. Devlin

We used to walk right by it every day,
  when the screws marched us from Death Row
    to the Exercise Yard
      between Block 8 and Block 9.
The first time I saw it,
  about a month after they'd transferred us
   from the old Charlestown bastille
     to the new joint at Walpole,
       I got shook up
         seeing it sitting there,
           a lot bigger than I'd imagined,
             waiting patiently for me.
"Fuck you!"
  I said to it as I swaggered by,
    playing the role,
      and one of the screws laughed.
I knew what he was thinking:
  "That bastard's got ice water in his veins
    instead of blood!"
He didn't know
  I could feel my asshole pucker up,

83

or that for a few horrible seconds
    I thought I'd shit my pants.
Later that night,
  and for too many other nights afterwards,
    I lay awake in the darkness of my cell,
       wondering how I would go
          when my time came
             to ride the lightning.
How I would feel
  as I sat in The Chair.
What I would say at the last moment.
How it would rank with other infamous last words.
"Warden, we've got to stop meeting like this. . . ."
"Does AC hurt less than DC?"
"Somebody . . . PLEASE! ! !"
"Don't forget, the governor wants my jockstrap!"
"Oh! I'm *not* on 'Candid Camera'?"
"Just keep holding my hand, warden. . . ."
"I'M INNOCENT! ! !"
"Is this trip necessary?"
SHAZAM! ! ! SHAZAM! ! ! SHAZAM! ! ! SHA. . . ."
"Are you *sure* that wasn't the telephone ringing?"
"YOU'RE ALL MOTHERFUCKERS! ! !"
"What a shocking experience *this* is going to be! ! !"
"But I didn't finish my Last Meal. . . ."
"Save me, warden, and I'll make you a good wife!"
"Look, a joke is a joke, but. . . ."
"HELP! ! ! !"
"I need to go to the toilet. . . ."
"I hope you guys like your meat well done!"
"NO, GOD! ! ! NO! ! !"
As things worked out,
  I never had to make up my mind
    exactly what to say.
I beat The Chair
  and got commuted to Life.

Looking back,
    I realize what a fool I was,
        in more ways than one.
No matter what I might have said,
    I would have been upstaged.
The Chair always has the last word.

The Routine

Arthur L. Devlin

".. . cleared 12 grand on that score!
Me and Wheels Magoo
   hit Vegas in my new Cadillac
    the very next day.
Man, what a blast!
(He sighs for effect)
Lasted almost three weeks
   before we hit Tap City.
(Shakes his head slowly)
Caddy and all—
   gonzo!
(Laughs softly)
What the fuck,
   easy come,
    easy go,
     right?
(Leans forward conspiratorially)
Know something?
   A week later
    I had plenty of bread again.
Punched a supermarket safe
   In Long Beach.

Single-O.
22 grand!
(Points a finger, winks)
That's when I started
    sockin' 10 percent away
        for a rainy day.
Every job I pulled
    from then on—
        Bang!—
            one-tenth of the loot
                right in the bank!
(Fumbles in his shirt pocket)
I still got
    a $300-a-month apartment out there,
        and a Lincoln Continental.
(Pats his pants pockets)
My chick's taking care of things
    until I hit the street again.
She sends me in a sawbuck a week.
Pays to look ahead, dig?
(Picks up his jacket, searches it, frowns)
Damn!
(Looks up, smiles disarmingly)
Say,
    you got a cigarette?
Guess I left mine in my cell . . ."

Back Gate Parole

Arthur L. Devlin

When I'd served sixteen months of my bit in San Quentin, thirteen of them in the notorious jute mill, the prison wheels called a temporary truce and assigned me to Q's Neumiller Hospital in July 1949. After having sweated over a hot loom in the mill for so long, my new job was a soft touch—clerk assistant to a Square John oculist from Frisco by the name of Meissner. The doc visited Quentin every Tuesday to take care of the cons, and that was the only day I worked. The rest of the week I took it easy, doing only what I wanted to do, either helping Ray Latshaw work on the stiffs in the morgue or sitting at my desk typing dirty stories I never dared let anyone else read.

Just as it takes all kinds of people to make a world, it takes all kinds of cons to make a prison. During the time I was at my station in the hospital clinic I saw more than my share of weirdos.

One morning, when the sick-call line was snaking through the clinic, I noticed that Dr. Kenny was tangled up with Cecil Giertz, a short, heavily built character who was always bugging the docs. This Giertz was a hypochondriac and never missed a day on sick call. He was all the time hitting the docs up for anything and everything for his imaginary ailments, like a special kind of oil to cure the dandruff in his eyebrows. Another time he asked for a pair of orthopedic shoes because he said the ones the state had issued him were so tight that his toenails were beginning to grow together.

After a few minutes with Giertz, Dr. Kenny began waving his arms around and his voice started to get loud. Not wanting to miss anything, I got up from my desk and sauntered on over to hear what was happening.

"For the last time, Giertz," Dr. Kenny was saying. "There is absolutely *nothing* wrong with your lip!"

Giertz put a hand up to his mouth and pulled his lower lip out like a Ubangi. "What's this, my imagination?" he yelled.

I moved in closer and leaned over to get a better look at Giertz's lower lip. There was a tiny sore spot on it. I looked at Dr. Kenny questioningly.

"If you're ready with your diagnosis, Dr. Devlin . . . ," Kenny said stiffly.

I stepped back out of the way. "Sorry, doc. I lost my head."

"Hope you find a better one!" he snapped.

"What about my lip?" Giertz cried. "How can you say there isn't anything wrong with it?"

Kenny smiled and patted Giertz's arm. "I mean that there is nothing *seriously* wrong with your lip. You've just picked up a little cold sore, that's all." He took out his pen and began writing on Giertz's sick-call card. "Now you take this over to the window there and get some salve and . . ."

"Salve!" Giertz broke in. *"Salve!* That ain't going to help me! You just don't want me to know I've got cancer!"

Chills shot up and down my spine at the mention of

that word. I've been bothered with cold sores all my life. One spot in particular, at the right-hand corner of my lower lip, is affected almost all the time. I'd always thought it was just one of those things, but Giertz started me wondering if maybe *I* had cancer all along and was just too stupid to know it! I was sorry I hadn't minded my own business.

"Oh, come now, Giertz!" Kenny said soothingly. "You don't have cancer!"

"Yes, I do! I can feel it working on my lip!"

I moved back a few steps, because Giertz's eyes were beginning to bulge and it looked as though he was going to get violent. Mr. Bell, the hospital screw, got up from his desk over by the door and grabbed Giertz by the arm.

"Okay, Giertz!" Bell said. "Move out!"

Giertz was trembling. "Nobody wants to help me! I've got cancer and all you people want to do is give me some damned salve!" He shot Dr. Kenny a dirty look and bolted out the door.

The following morning, Giertz was back on the sick-call line, this time telling his tale of woe to Dr. Grayson, who'd drawn the clinic duty for the day. Dr. Grayson gave Giertz some more salve—or tried to.

Over the course of the week I noticed that Giertz hit on every doc on the staff. Finally, to pacify him, Dr. Leo L. Stanley, Quentin's chief medical officer, took a tiny sliver of tissue from Giertz's lip and sent the specimen to an outside lab for examination.

Three days later the report came back that Giertz was okay. No cancer. Dr. Stanley called him in that same day and showed him the slip stamped "Negative," explaining exactly what it meant. Giertz didn't say a word. He just listened, glared at everybody in sight, and then stormed out of the clinic.

I sort of forgot about Cecil Giertz for the next couple of days, having problems of my own, like trying to think up new plots for my dirty stories. Then one afternoon I went up to the gym to play some ping-pong with a buddy of mine who worked up there, Freddy Korst. In those days the Quentin gym was up on the top floor of the old Industrial Building, three stories above the ground. Freddy and I were in the middle of a wild game when suddenly we heard a lot of yelling going on down in the Alley below.

"Massey's after somebody again," Freddy said. Massey was the screw in charge of the Alley, and it was his job to stop the cons from sneaking up to the gym during working hours. He wouldn't let his own mother up to the gym without a pass.

I heard Massey shout: "Hey! Stop! You can't go up there unless you have a pass!"

I could hear someone running up the steps. I stopped playing and looked over toward the doorway just as Cecil Giertz came charging through it. He leaned against the wall to catch his breath. He was bent over, his arms swinging back and forth, head up, his eyes rolling crazily, and his mouth was twisted sideways as if he was trying to imitate Charles Laughton playing the hunchback of Notre Dame.

Massey yelled again. "Hey! You up there in the gym! If you don't get down here right away I'm coming up after you!"

Giertz didn't move.

"Okay, if that's the way you want it!" Massey's footsteps sounded on the iron stairs.

I was still watching Giertz. He straightened up, and his eyes met mine. I didn't like what I saw.

When Massey was almost at the top of the stairs, Giertz suddenly started running across the gym toward my end of the ping-pong table. For one frightening moment I thought he was coming after me, but then he was past me and heading for one of the open windows and it was too late to stop him. He put his arms up as though he was diving off a springboard into a swimming pool, and without breaking stride he went headfirst out of the window.

"Jesus H. Christ!" Freddy said.

I hurried on over to the window and looked down. Giertz had landed on his face beside a pile of lumber stacked up outside of the carpenter shop. I turned away from the window, brushed past Massey, who was standing in the middle of the gym floor with a puzzled expression on his face, and ran down the stairs and around to the back of the Industrial Building. When I reached Giertz, two cons were standing beside his body, looking down at him. I was amazed that there wasn't any blood visible.

One of the cons shook his head. "He's had it, man!"

A crowd quickly gathered. I waited around until a couple of my buddies from the hospital arrived. I helped them pick Giertz up and put him on a gurney, face up. His forehead was caved in just a little, and there was a trickle of blood coming from his nose. I bent over him for a second and I could see that little sore spot still there in the right-hand corner of his lower lip.

After supper that night, as we waited on the top tier of the South Block "B" Section to be let back into our cages, four or five of us were cutting up the events of the day. The main topic of conversation was Cecil Giertz.

My cell partner, Bob Dixon, said, "Nobody wants out of this joint more than I do, but I ain't about to take a 'Back Gate Parole.'"

Quentin's cemetery is located less than a mile outside the rear gate of the prison, up on a hillside overlooking the bay. Most of the cons who die while serving time end up there, unwanted by their families or relations, and any guy who left that way was labeled with the obvious tag.

"He had to be crazy," Jim Luxton said.

Dixon laughed. "At least his troubles are over. No strain, no pain." He hit me on the shoulder. "Right, Dev? Here you are with a bundle of time left to do, and ol' Giertz hasn't got a thing to worry about now."

"You're right," I said, looking down over the railing at the cement floor of the block, some ninety feet below, and thinking of all those long years ahead of me. "Maybe he wasn't so crazy after all."

A Nose By Any Other Name . . .

Arthur L. Devlin

I had a cell partner
  in San Quentin
  who drove me bananas.
He was always picking his nose.
Three months was enough for me
I finally had to get a Cell Change.
No matter what else he was doing—
    just laying on his lower bunk,
      or playing dominoes,
        or taking a shit,
          or eating next to me in the mess hall—
            he was always picking his nose.
That wasn't so bad by itself,
  but one night,
    just before Lights-Out,
      I leaned out over my bunk
      and saw him
        eating that gooky stuff
          he'd just dug out of his nose!
From then on,
  I really kept the peek on him.

At least two or three times a day
   I'd catch him
      licking snots off his finger,
         or chomping away
            on the thick, hard, stringy stuff,
               really enjoying himself.
Like I said,
   I finally had to move out.
It got to be too much for me.
Three months with that creep!
And every day
   him eating that stuff
      he got out of his nose
         and never *once* offering me any!

Harrison and Campbell

Arthur L. Devlin

They died together,
  side by side
    in San Quentin's
      twin Gas Chamber chairs
        one quiet Friday morning,
      unable to digest
        a late breakfast
          of cyanide eggs
            dipped in acid.

Two young black men
  I'd met in the L.A. County Jail,
    where we were being held
      in the High-Power tanks
      under top security,
        back in 1947.

They were in 10-A-2
  on a holdup-murder beef,
    and I was in 10-A-1
      on armed robbery charges
      and attempted escape.

We used to rap
  in the cage
    just off the Attorney Room,
      while waiting for visits
        with our Public Defenders.

We got to know each other fairly well,
  and I liked them both.

Then they got hit with Murder One
  and left for Q's Death Row.

I followed them to the joint
  on a five-to-life
    a few months later.

The last time we met
  was in the Quentin morgue,
    where they were brought
      on the afternoon of the day
        they were topped.

I was working in the hospital,
  and Ray Latshaw
    let me in to see them
      for the final go-round.

They looked a lot smaller,
  stretched out on the slabs.

Know what I remember most
  about them
    after all these years?

No one
  even bothered to come to the prison
    to pick up their bodies.

JOANNE E. TIDD

*Alderson Federal Reformatory for Women,
Alderson, West Virginia*

Joanne is a twenty-four-year-old flower
with thorns who is serving what is known at
Alderson as a "zip-six" (six months to six
years) for conspiracy to distribute schedule-
one narcotics. Joanne is a delightful pain in
the ass who would rather raise hell than eat,
but that is far from her total makeup and
she simply needs to run into Mr. Right Dude,
with the sugar-coated bit and the soft-soled
butt boots. The aforementioned, employed
properly by the right guy, mixed regularly
with genuine love and concern, will assure
him that there won't be much else in life he
will need.

A Letter to the President

September 20, 1972

Mr. Richard M. Nixon
1600 Pennsylvania Avenue, N.W.
Washington, D.C.

Dear Sir:

I am an inmate at the Alderson Federal Reformatory for Women. I am doing what we call a "zip-six," six months to six years, under the Youth Correctional Act. When I was sentenced the judge talked a lot about rehabilitation and rehabilitational programs, but I can't find any here. Where are they at?

When a woman first arrives here, her first instincts are to straighten up and try to become a part of the "establishment," but it isn't long before her attitude changes. For example, if I was released today I would probably obey society's laws, but not out of respect or fear, rather out of disgust and hatred.

I used to love this country, until I went through its courts and came here, until I saw what America the Beautiful does to keep its subjects in line. I don't want to dislike the United States, even now, but this institution's "mind games" are tearing apart my convictions about truth and justice.

After talking with several other girls here, I have found out that I was not alone in my thinking and I have come to realize several things: Judges simply don't know what they are sentencing people to when they hand out time. Those righteous men, sitting behind benches, enshrouded in flowing black robes, think they are sending people to places of rehabilitation, when in truth they would do better sending people to a horse farm or something of the like. All we get is indifference, scorn and threats from the staff members here and we are treated mostly like idiots. I overheard one girl say, "They must think I checked my brains at the gate on the way in." I won't mention this girl's name because I don't want to get her in any trouble, but she has two years of college under her belt.

Sure, to the casual observer, Alderson is beautiful, with trees, flowers and vine-covered cottages. Nor will anyone see a wall surrounding the grounds or watchtowers and gun-toting guards, but all walls don't have to be made of stone. The walls here are made out of tension, hatred, fear and isolation, and are far more formidable than any bricks or stones. I've learned one lesson well since I have been here, and it deals with survival. I have learned how to hate, though I never hated anything before. I have learned how to be suspicious of anyone and anything, though I used to trust people at first sight. I know, too, that when I die I will surely go to heaven, because I am doing my stint in hell right now. I was twenty years old and a junkie when I was sent here, and perhaps I wasn't the best example of "young society," but I never hurt anyone. By the time I leave I will in all probability be a "penitentiary turnout," another product of the American penal system.

I truly hope I am explaining things, though I doubt

it, because the only real way to understand prison is to become a part of it. That way you can learn what makes a person into a cold, unfeeling individual, instead of a productive member of society. That way you could experience the frustration of trying to get help from one of these administrators or staff members, who are for the most part "just putting in their eight hours."

I don't really believe that you are concerned about what happens to me or any of the other five hundred or so girls here at Alderson, but I thought I would at least grab at a straw. We know we are society's outcasts, packed away to the mountains, far from family and friends, to be forgotten, but there are some here who still hope that "our government" is still "our government" and that we haven't been alienated totally from the people that it is supposed to stand by in the face of wrong and injustice.

I don't have much more to write, because now that I have reached this point in my letter, I have come to the conclusion that I am wasting my time. Yet, at least I can say I cared enough to try. I wonder if you can say the same.

Sincerely,
Joanne E. Tidd #19121
Alderson FRW
Box A
Alderson, West Virginia

P.S.
Please answer this letter, so I will know that you received it . . .

JODI JEANNE HARRIS

Alderson Federal Reformatory for Women
Alderson, West Virginia

Jodi is *the* hell raiser of hell raisers in Alderson, being transferred out on various occasions to Detroit House of Correction and Cooke County Jail. Yet if someone merely takes the time to look beneath the veneer of toughness, a sensitivity and warmth worth its weight in gold will be exposed. As of this writing, Jodi is going through a program called "The Steps," which is a six-week, self-evaluation-isolation setup. It took her four weeks to graduate from Step One, and one can't help wondering, with an affectionate grin, how many years it will take her to complete the six-week program. Jodi hails from Peoria, Illinois, and the light of her life is a two-year-old gem named Wendy.

A Letter to the Director of
the Bureau of Prisons

November 25, 1972

Dear Mr. Carlson:

My name is Jodi Jeanne Harris #19183 and I am presently an inmate in the Federal Women's Reformatory at Alderson, West Virginia. There are several things that I would like to bring to your attention, for the betterment of the prisoners incarcerated here at Alderson, so that at least we will have a fighting chance to become useful citizens, once we step back out into society.

My primary purpose for writing to you is not to reveal any gory facts or details (though I have some), but to try to interest you enough to either come here and talk to me yourself, or send someone with an open mind to listen to the grievances. It has long been obvious that there is no help or understanding forthcoming from the Alderson staff members, case workers or guards. They simply aren't interested in how we feel, and the replies to bona fide grievances are threats of lock-in, transfers, etc., if we don't shut up.

There are many things I could say and *prove,* but the only way I would speak out in detail is to someone

107

with the authority to make changes and to guarantee the safety of myself and others who might step forward.

On behalf of myself and the other women who are in your charge at Alderson, I beseech you to give us the opportunity to be heard.

Thank you in advance for your time and consideration.

> Sincerely,
> Jodi Jeanne Harris #19183
> Alderson FRW
> Box A
> Alderson, West Virginia

LETTER FROM ALDERSON

Anonymous

A Letter to the Commissioner on
Civil Rights

January 11, 1973

Mr. Howard A. Glickman
Staff Director
Commission on Civil Rights
1405 Eye Street
Washington, D.C. 20425

Dear Mr. Glickman:

I have heard about you through a friend of mine, along with her problems concerning the mail here at Alderson Federal Reformatory for Women. I too am having problems, as my boyfriend receives my mail, but I don't get his. For some time now I had thought that he simply decided not to correspond with me anymore, but he sent a message, through the visitor of a friend, that he has been writing almost every day but his letters keep coming back with a stamped finger, stating "Return to sender." They have all been going back, while no one even thought enough of me to let me know that any had ever arrived.

Is there anything you or your organization could do to help myself and the others in here? I and the entire population would greatly appreciate any aid or assistance in this area. Can you see the harm in writing to *anyone?* We all understand the necessity for screening visitors to the institution, but what damage could possibly be done hundreds or thousands of miles apart?

The mail situation here is a complete disaster. Letters from others, from anywhere, mean a great deal to those of us who are limited to prison grounds and confines. Help stamp out a little loneliness, won't you please?

Please respond, if only to let me know that you received this letter.

Sincerely,
Anonymous
Alderson FRW
Box A
Alderson, West Virginia

THREE LETTERS TO ALDERSON

H. H. McKernan

Reply to
A Letter to the President

UNITED STATES DEPARTMENT OF JUSTICE
Bureau of Prisons
Washington 20537

November 8, 1972

Ms. Joanne E. Tidd
Reg. No. 19121-170
Box A
Alderson, West Virginia 24910
Dear Ms. Tidd:

I have your recent letter to the President of the United States, and the matter about which you are concerned is one which should be brought to the attention of the institution staff. I am, therefore, returning your letter so the appropriate staff member can review it with you and take any action that may be warranted. Your Case Manager or Correctional Counselor will be glad to discuss this matter with you and to assist you with a solution to your problems, or he may possibly refer you to another member of the staff.

Sincerely,

H. H. McKERNAN
Chief, Case Management

Reply to
A Letter to the Director of
the Bureau of Prisons

UNITED STATES DEPARTMENT OF JUSTICE
Bureau of Prisons
Washington 20537

November 29, 1972

Ms. Jodi Jeanne Harris
Reg. No. 19183-170
Box A
Alderson, West Virginia 24910
Dear Ms. Harris:

I have your recent letter to the Director of the Bureau of Prisons and the matter about which you are concerned is one which should be brought to the attention of the institution staff. I am, therefore, returning your letter so the appropriate staff member can review it with you and take any action that may be warranted. Your Case Manager or Correctional Counselor will be glad to discuss this matter with you and to assist you with a solution to your problem, or he may possibly refer you to another member of the staff.

Sincerely,

H. H. McKERNAN
Chief, Case Management

Reply to
A Letter to
the Commissioner on Civil Rights

UNITED STATES DEPARTMENT OF JUSTICE
Bureau of Prisons
Washington 20537

January 22, 1973

Ms. Anonymous
Reg. No. Anonymous
Box A
Alderson, West Virginia 24910
Dear Ms. Anonymous:

I have your recent letter to the Director of the
Commission on Civil Rights and the matter about
which you are concerned is one which should be
brought to the attention of the institution staff. I am,
therefore, returning your letter so the appropriate staff
member can review it with you and take any action
that may be warranted. Your Case Manager or Correctional Counselor will be glad to discuss this matter
with you and to assist you with a solution to your
problem, or he may refer you to another member of
the staff.

Sincerely,
H. H. McKERNAN
Chief, Case Management

MARGUERITE FERRANTE

California Institution for Women, Frontera, California

Marguerite is a fiery young lady, who has a reputation around the penal circuit for telling it like she sees it. Her piece, "A Turtle's Tale," is an ideal cram course in how to get the hell out of jail, but she is deeply involved in the plight of women prisoners, proving it regularly with a steady stream of enlightening articles.

A Turtle's Tale

Marguerite Ferrante

This turtle came by chance to prison, and was told she would have to stay. Since she couldn't leave, she decided to look around her and see what was what and it wasn't long before she started learning the games of prison. Some games were played for fun. Some games were played for real. Some games were played for blood. During this learning period, the incarcerated turtle was used, bruised and stepped on time and time again.

Yet with every lesson she learned a little, and eventually learned how to pull in her head, arms and legs, whenever things got out of hand. By sliding up under her shell, she learned that she didn't have to suffer the whims of man or woman.

Pretty soon this prison turtle had mastered the art of "not making any waves." She had learned to watch, to read in advance the people and their games, and she learned how to avoid being the object of these games. She knew not to get involved, because your involvement would only be turned around and used against you. She knew not to carry any load but her own, thus avoiding being labeled a "trick" by her peers and by the staff. She knew to listen when some-one was speaking, but only until an opportunity came to leave. She also learned how to say the things others wanted to hear, rather than let them know her true feelings.

Her final lesson revealed that no one really cared enough to wonder why she didn't grow, why she simply remained beneath her shell and died a little each day.

It shouldn't be this way, but because of the well-learned lessons, this little turtle will probably survive her journey through the prison.

LEROY BONNER

Rahway State Prison, Rahway, New Jersey

Leroy started doing time in 1945 at age fourteen. He graduated from a state home for boys in 1950, moving on up the line to a reformatory for older boys. After returning twice to the penal systems' preparatory school he was transferred to still another reformatory, another rung on the penal ladder. He finally made it to Trenton State Prison in 1954, and after revolving in and out three times, finally returned with a thirty-year bid, which he is currently serving. He was transferred to Rahway State Prison in 1971. His article is unedited, except for the "d's", which he writes backwards. He is forty-one years old.

How a Homo Fill

Leroy Bonner

My name is Leroy Bonner I am 41 I have bin
a homo for 33 yere I red 2 or 3 book an i fill some
ar good an bad some people fill dat homo ar sick
my friend an i talk about dis all the time for 33 yere
my life i no homo come frome a lot of ding many
homo come frome children day do not git love frome
dere dad and mother most dad do not cere whot
dere boy do boy leren homo acts when dere goen
on day leren frome ather boy some dad to gay have
sun dat ar homo dat aren ahwere who gay when i
wus a boy i have acts begalls i thing my mother do not
love me a homo is happy or lonly dere ar 5 given
cine homo 1 tipe stan on a corner to cit pigd up the
act begalls gay fill day mite cit rejeted gay fill that
nobody love then so most man dat are homo
  the same boy do not leren act frome homos 1
boy stay over nite whith his boy fran the act has
been dat nite i no dat boy was me 9 out of 10
boy dat ar homo starit dat way you will fine boy
frome 7 to 19 all over ustate out on the toun loocking
to be pigd up some do not cit pigd up dey have a
good time when dere boy fran home he tell his da

he have a good time so dat wy i say some dad an mother do not no dere boy dere are meny mor dings to tell about homo i whood rite a book but i cant rite to good no man shood rite about homo homo are the only uns dat no about dat life i am gona rite a book about 400 pabes an i will tell very ding on homo life i no i ben 1 for 33 yere thank you for reading this

paragraf 2

i never have wman in my life i have bin in an out jail all my life over 20 yere out of 41 yere i never have a shansh to make out whith a wman makby i whas a frade ar i never cear wen i was in a boy home at 9 yere old sex act beginnit i fill lollny so i jion dem in the acts i fill love wen it all my life i have sex and love misxed up now dat i no whot love is a fillin dat you have for some un all homo have a femal tenzy in dem

paragraf 3

whot a boy wunt a boy wunt love an avekshun frome his dad an mother some dad do not cear whot dere sun do dat wy a boy do not cear whot he do he is like athr boy dat boy do homo sex acts an drugs an meny more ding day do begawze day do not git the love shood git boy fill asifit with ather boy a boy well do eny ding whith his boy frand to be if a boy stele a car his boy fran well go whith him to do it all boils doun to whot i sade befor

paragraf 4

peeple shood gift love shood love suns not beet dem dat whot make dem bad mother shood unstan

wy dere sun shood love dem   gib dem hell an do
not beet dem   an you will fine the boy well love
you bak

JACK FITZPATRICK

Rahway State Prison, Rahway, New Jersey

In sixteen of his thirty-eight years, Jack did time in various prisons around the country; Lewisburg, Huntsville, Leavenworth, Trenton and Rahway. He was at the Springfield Medical Center for dental surgery when he met Robert Stroud, better known as The Birdman of Alcatraz. Jack was scheduled for some "streetside" seven months ago, and on the way out I asked him if he had been rehabilitated. "Not so much rehabilitated as wore out," he replied.

A few months ago he was executed gangland style in Newark, New Jersey.

The Death of the Birdman

Jack Fitzpatrick

In the latter part of August 1963, I met and talked for the first time with one of the most controversial prisoners of this century. Robert Stroud was his name, but he was better known as The Birdman of Alcatraz. To convicts and officials, he was a living legend.

At the time of our meeting I was transferred to the United States Medical Center for Federal Prisoners at Springfield, Missouri, for a series of dental operations. Upon my arrival there, I found myself on the same floor as this famed convict. It was hard to believe that the slow-moving, stoop-shouldered old man standing before me, offering me a cigarette, was really the infamous Birdman of Alcatraz. It didn't seem humanly possible that the giant I knew of had deteriorated into this skeleton of a man.

We talked briefly about inconsequential things, with him doing most of the talking. I soon found out that this was his favorite pastime. The long years of solitude had made him willing to converse with anyone, anywhere, any time of the day or night—anyone other than custodial officials. He hated all guards with a passion I have never seen evidenced by any other human being. Perhaps in his mind he had sufficient cause, for the only humans he could talk to during forty-seven years of solitary confinement were guards.

He was committed to McNeils Island Penitentiary in 1907 with a five-year sentence for manslaughter. He was nineteen years old at the time, bitter, and became a disciplinary problem to the administration. Subsequently he was transferred to Leavenworth. In 1909 he killed a guard at Leavenworth—a guard who refused his mother permission to visit him. The guard told his mother that visiting hours were over and that she would have to return the following month. This created quite a problem, since she had traveled from Alaska. Stroud felt that the guard was denying him his visiting privileges and killed him. As a result, he was tried, found guilty and sentenced to be hanged. This sentence was eventually commuted to an even more inhumane one—ninety-nine years in solitary confinement!

At the time of our meeting, Stroud was seventy-three years old. Forty-seven of those years he had spent by himself. I saw or spoke to him at least once on every day of the four months that I knew him. At times he would talk at great length and I would listen. It wasn't that he wouldn't listen, because his faculties were sound and he would remember everything that was said to him, but I think he liked to do the talking because he was just a lonely old man who grew up in solitary, changed from a boy to a man with no one but himself to converse with. Naturally, he derived his greatest pleasure in having someone just listen to him.

At first I took him to be a senile old man, but the more he talked, the more I began to think differently. True, his body was torn down, but his mind was clear and alert. Stroud could converse fluently in German, French, Spanish or English. He was a self-taught mathematician and was familiar with all forms of calculus. It was astonishing when one considered that he had only a sixth-grade formal education.

It was in Leavenworth that Stroud first became interested in birds. Starting with one fledgling sparrow that had fallen from its nest, along with many long and bitter feuds with prison officials, he managed to become the foremost authority on bird diseases in the world. Contrary to popular belief, Stroud never had a bird in Alcatraz! All of his work with birds was done in Leavenworth. His transfer to Alcatraz in 1942 came for two reasons. The first was due to public opinion, as congressmen, philanthropists and the public were slowly coming around to aid Stroud in his fight for freedom. James V. Bennet, then director of the Federal Bureau of Prisons, ordered Stroud transferred to Alcatraz; the most isolated federal prison in the world.

For thirty years Stroud had done nothing but improve himself. He discovered unheard-of ways to combat bird diseases and in doing so, helped countless numbers of bird lovers throughout the world. In short, he had turned himself into a useful and productive member of society. Still, one night, with his freedom almost in sight, two U.S. marshals removed him from his "home" and his birds at Leavenworth and transferred him to Alcatraz. According to Stroud, Bennet's reasoning was twofold. The first was to remove him from any association or contact with the public. On "The Rock" he would have no chance to communicate with anybody. The second reason for the transfer was that Stroud was making quite a bit of money through the sales of his book and his articles on the curing of bird diseases. The Bureau of Prisons, again acting on orders from Bennet, ordered the discontinuing of federal prisoners earning money from the free world. However, this edict came only after Bennet had sent an emissary to see Stroud with an offer: If Stroud would turn over 50 percent of his earnings to the

Bureau of Prisons, he would be permitted to continue his research on birds. Stroud refused and as a result his birds were taken from him and he was transferred to "The Rock."

Stroud often told me that he believed he would have been a free man had not James Bennet been director of the Bureau of Prisons. Stroud and the director carried on their personal feud, with neither giving an inch, until the day that Stroud died. It may be noted that shortly after Stroud's death, James V. Bennet retired from the bureau.

Stroud didn't like too many people. He would talk with anyone, but he only liked a few. With the passing of time, I came to like the old man and I felt that he also liked me. He always addressed me as "Mister," as he did every other prisoner. He once told me, on the subject of confinement: "The real punishment of being confined in any prison is the loss of dignity and individuality that a man is forced to endure." It wasn't difficult to understand his proud disposition. He wore it wherever he went.

There was a myth created by Hollywood in their motion picture of Stroud's life, that he helped quell the 1954 riot on "The Rock." The picture showed the National Guard being called in and Stroud throwing the guns out the window to them, telling the warden that there were no more guns in the cell block. Stroud didn't like this and told me the incident never happened. From 1942 until 1959 he was kept in segregation, a closed unit with single cells next to the hospital. The riot took place in "D" cell block on the other side of the yard; a good way off from where Stroud was housed. Often this man told me the true stories of the many myths that had been created around him, and that was the one he disliked the most.

One night, shortly before lights out, Stroud came to my cell and asked me to go to the recreation room

134

with him. Rarely did I ever see him go anywhere alone, but this was the first time he came and asked me to go with him. It was the first time I ever saw him express a negative attitude. He talked and I listened.

In the past, every time a man was scheduled for release, Stroud was the first to wish him luck, but he became irate after reading an article about Nathan Leopold who was paroled from Joliet Prison. His partner, Loeb, had been killed by another inmate while in prison many years earlier.

Stroud believed their case was far more notorious than his, because they had killed for thrills, selecting a complete stranger. Now one of them was a free man.

"Look at this newspaper clipping," Stroud said to me. "This guy killed for kicks. At least I felt that the people I killed had wronged me. Where is the justice?" He was almost childlike in his jealousy of Leopold. "You know, all these years I believed that someday I would get out, but now I don't know. I just don't know. . . ." He might have had some premonition for he remarked, "I hope I don't die behind the walls."

It was the only time during the four months that I knew him that he ever projected a defeatist attitude. For a man who had endured what he had, this seemed to undermine his whole being. Fortunately this attitude did not last long.

During the next few weeks I began to notice that he was watching me closely. Everywhere I went, the library, the television room, the ball field, the Birdman was always somewhere in the vicinity. Finally one day he stopped me.

"Come to my room after chow. I have something to show you."

That night I went to his room and as I walked in, he smiled and pulled out of his locker one of the thickest manuscripts I have ever seen. There were thousands of pages, all written in longhand, hardly legible. He told me how he had spent years gathering and preparing this material and that every word written was the gospel truth. He explained how he began writing it in Leavenworth, adding to it during his stay in Alcatraz and Springfield. I'll never know how he managed to keep it in his possession because whenever I asked him he kept changing the subject. Probably his reason for not telling me was his distrust of almost everyone. He did let me read parts of it, though he never permitted me to leave his room with the manuscript.

His writings described in detail the entire federal system of incarceration. It was the true story of the Bureau of Prisons, of the people who staffed the various prisons before and after the formation of the Bureau of Prisons. He named names, dates, places, circumstances, events; the whole development of the bureau from 1935 to 1963. It was all there—the good and the bad. . . .

There were several publishing firms that Stroud had written to, telling them of the existence of his manuscript. He showed me letters that were sent to his attorney from all the companies that wanted to publish the material. Stroud, of course, had no way of sending it to them.

Finally in 1963 he took the matter to court under a writ of habeas corpus and in Springfield, Missouri, he made an effort to secure a court order that would permit him to have the manuscript published. This was in November, and after two days of deliberation the court decided not to release the manuscript on the grounds that it was detrimental to the public welfare. The court also decided that the manuscript was against prison regulations and ordered that it be turned over to the Medical Center authorities.

Stroud returned to the Medical Center and oddly enough it wasn't his defeat in court that he talked about, but about how different it felt to walk in a town again, even though he was handcuffed and under armed guard. His natural optimism, the ability to pass off setbacks as minute happenings, overwhelmed me. There was no bitterness in his voice when he told me: "Someday it will be published."

Stroud had formerly worked in the bookbinding section of the library, but now his failing health did not even permit that limited activity. He was placed on a special diet and spent most of his time in his room. Whenever I did pass his room he would smile and wave cheerfully but no longer did he speak or invite me in.

It was about this time that I was scheduled for dental surgery. Due to the delicacy of the operation, I was placed on medication every four hours. About midnight, November 20, 1963, while receiving my medication, I saw Stroud approach the officer on duty. He told the guard that he had sharp shooting pains around his left shoulder and that his arm was numb. He asked to see the doctor, but the guard told him it wasn't possible and to put his name on sick call in the morning.

The Birdman drew himself erect and said: "I should have known better than to ask a hack for anything." Then he turned to me and said, "So long, kid."

I looked at him for a long moment, puzzled. He had never called me anything but "Mister." No longer could I see his face, but as I watched him move off tiredly, I thought of the tremendous will to live, the unbending spirit that had carried him through forty-seven heart-breaking years of solitary confinement. The only discernible difference was that his courage could no longer sustain his failing body. Little did I suspect that his farewell words to me were probably the last he said to any man.

At approximately six-thirty the news reached me.

137

Stroud had died in his sleep. It is difficult, even now, to describe how I and the other prisoners felt. He had endured so much and we all thought he would live forever.

The institution did not release the news of Stroud's death until after they had a chance to perform an autopsy. This wasn't concluded until the following day, November 22, 1963, and the Springfield newspapers were notified. By then, the world was interested in the death of another man, John F. Kennedy, who had been assassinated in Dallas, Texas. Stroud's passing went practically unnoticed.

Robert Stroud, The Birdman of Alcatraz, was as unlucky in death as he was in life.

MARY VANGI

California Institution for Women, Frontera, California

Passing the Time Away

Mary Vangi

A dedication is in order: To the Lonesome Crow, Blind Speculator, Winger Wonder, Super Seer and other words for the same song: Earth women at CIW, while finding the ground, grass and trees a good place to be from, still hold words from Johnny Cash's song, "But flesh and blood needs flesh and blood," to be kin to the Gospel Truth. We've had an extended spring here, mistaking starlings of unusual size and confidence for crows, blackbirds and other love things, seen reality in a flash while stumbling, and changed the outlook of things on the inside. With flowers all planted and watered, it left not much to do but "Sing you a song not very long, gonna sing it right, if it takes all night" and turn our thoughts to mushrooms and mysterious writers that live on mountain tops. . . . End of dedication, it would seem, but not really. . . .

Meanwhile, back in the guppy bowl, it's really hot summer. Summer means watermelon and flies, corn-on-the-cob and flies, sunbathing and flies, evening campus privileges and flies, outdoor entertainment and flies. . . . I wonder what the builders and planners had on their minds when they constructed a women's prison

141

right next to a cow farm? Some mornings I expect to wake up and find the first word out of my mouth to be "Moo-oo-o" just like those Learn-a-Language-While-You-Sleep records. Wonder how much money I could make talking to cows for a living? Helping out farmers with milking problems—"Moo-oo-o." "Well, Mr. J. Citizen, that means Bessie doesn't like the spray you put on the grass yesterday—it makes her hostile." "Moo-oo-oo-oo-oo." "Well, Mrs. J. Citizen, Bessie resents your daughter naming her doll after her. She says it's degrading because the doll is only plastic." I think I'll go through the meal line tonight "moo-oo-o-ing" at the staff. "No, Mrs. V., I'm not being disrespectful, I'm learning a trade."

It's as good a trip as any, besides, it's not hurting anyone—not even me! I figured it all out today: Two more Christmases, two more birthdays, one more Fourth of July and if I'm lucky, only one more Easter before I'm home. Seems like a long month, that's all. You know, God, when you decided to let us humans figure out things like TIME into days, months, years and hours, you forgot about a way to include our feelings, thoughts and living into the calendar. So next time you create a world, God, would you either get the TIME thing straight or leave it out entirely, please? Thanks.

DR. THOMAS COX

Glassboro State College, Glassboro, New Jersey

Yes, Virginia, you read it right. Dr. Cox is currently an assistant professor at Glassboro State College in New Jersey. He no longer sports a prison number, but he had several, serving time in facilities such as Atlanta, Leavenworth and Michigan State Prison. He teaches a course called "Law and Justice" and even after all this time still doesn't feel that he has managed to dig out of the mire of his past. In a letter to me he wrote: "After each day's excavation, I look about and usually see that the sides of my hole have caved right back in on me again." It just goes to show that sometimes the label goes on *before* the quality goes in!

The Black Stomps

Thomas Cox

The black boots glistened in the pawnshop window. Mel stood on the sidewalk fascinated by them. They would be just the things to set off his bike rig. The black leather jacket and whipcord pistol pants didn't seem right with blue suede shoes—all right for the corner, but not for a wheel man.

The shop bell tinkled and Mel stood before Sid.

"Can I do something for you, my boy?"

"Yeah, man, what's the tariff on those black stomps?"

"Black—what!"

"Black stomps—the bike boots, Pop, the bike boots."

"Certainly, certainly, the black boots in the window. I should have known."

Sid's business brought him in contact with many weird characters, but these hipsters were always the zaniest. Best to make the sale and get rid of the kid. Who knows? He might be hopped up on dope and decide to wreck the place.

"The boots are eighteen dollars."

"Six, seven, eight, wrap 'em up, Pop."

"Just a minute, boy, I clearly said eighteen dollars, not eight."

"I heard you say eight bills, Pop. Now wrap 'em up."

He was one of the wild ones all right. Glassy eyes. DA haircut. The works. Might go amuck. But Sid had to be firm.

"Eighteen dollars, son, or no boots."

Mel's eyes glinted for a second. He couldn't stand being repulsed, especially by this old toad with the heavy peepers.

"Okay, Pop, the eighteen big ones are yours. Now, deliver me the stomps."

Sid hesitated. What's worrying me? Can't let this kid frighten me. What have I got this .32 automatic in my pocket for? He thumped the boots on the counter.

"Crazy man, real crazy, but Pop, you're killing my stash."

Another gleam flickered in Mel's eyes. What would the troops think when they picked up on these stomps? He had to have them but replacing the eighteen bills involved some risks. Besides, his broad liked to travel first class. Couldn't do that paying out this kind of scratch for footwear. Well, he was Mel Warner, big-time operator. A wheel man! His twisted mental gears gnashed.

"Say, man, did you ever think that some dark night a wheel job might just crash through your window, or maybe a fire might start? All accidental, you understand, man, but it could happen. It'd be too bad if you didn't have insurance, now wouldn't it, Pop?" Mel was sure of himself. He knew that most of these creeps were too tight to insure.

Sid's anger was up, but he was much older and wiser than Mel. So the kid wanted to try a little extortion. So what! He did have insurance, so why waste time

146

worrying about it. The kid might act crazy, but he'd never pull a stunt like that.

"I said eighteen dollars, son. Either the money or no boots." His tone registered finality.

Years of unrestrained impulses formulated Mel's next action. He was king of the Green Street Counts. He and his crew took what they wanted. Take the boots, then! Who was this rag of an old man?

Sid's pudgy fingers grasped Mel's sleeve as he turned to flee. Whirling, with the ferocity of an enraged bull, Mel crashed the heavy boots into Sid's forehead.

The punk's done it! Got to get my gun out! Can't move my hand! That pain! That maniac screaming!

"Five, six, seven, uh, eight, yeah, Pop, you'll get eighteen big ones all right, twelve, thirteen, yeah, man, eighteen big ones—big lumps that is."

On the way to the floor, Sid's head crunched against the marble counter edge and brought him merciful relief.

"He's dead, captain. His skull's a real mess. Can't understand it. Not a cent seems to be missing. Nothing has been touched. If robbery was the motive, the killer must have been scared off. Lady that found Steinberg said he whispered something about a crazy kid and "black boots."

"I know, sergeant, I know. Put out a citywide alarm. Round up every pair of 'boots' in town. Start with that bunch on Green Street. Our boy's probably there."

STOMP SLAYER SEIZED! The trial was almost as brief as the headlines, although the papers got more grist for their mill when the judge, a kindly, conscientious jurist, addressed Mel personally.

"Son, would you please tell the court just what occurred between you and the deceased?"

"Pop, you'll have to break that down. I don't dig you."

The judge remained calm. Long ago he had become familiar with the actions and the strange street language of the city's adolescents. Using great restraint, he spoke quietly to Mel.

"Very well, son. Would you please tell me why you killed Mr. Steinberg?"

The time had come. Mel was ready. "It's like this, Pop. I hit the shop for my stomps when this lame comes off with some static. So I chill him, but quick. Get me, man?"

The courtroom was a babble. From among the spectators' section, members of the Counts shouted words of encouragement to Mel. Others in attendance were visibly shaken at the flippant and callous description of the murder. The court was less than pleased with the loss of dignity in the proceedings.

The judge spoke sharply. "Young man, do you realize that you are in a court of law, answering to a charge of murder? Surely you can speak with some appreciation of the English language, considering the gravity of your situation."

"I ain't diggin, you, Pop!" Mel spat back. "You're too far away. In fact, man, you're so far away I can't even see you!"

The courtroom turned into bedlam. Mel took it all in and felt good. Yeah, it was kicks, real kicks! All the Green Street Counts had showed up, and the dolls. His doll was there. What a mob! Any guy would be proud of a solid crew like the Counts. Real inspirational! He raised his voice in ranting fury.

"This whole morgue's phony. A giant creep joint."

Mel's supporters roared. The judge's gavel rose and fell. Bam! Bam! Bailiffs began ejecting the raucous Counts from the courtroom. The remaining spectators grew silent.

Mel was proud of himself. Just look at those creeps! What a bunch of squares. There was reason to be proud. Here he was, number-one guy, the star of the show. He was cool. His hair marcelled. Sideburns long and curly. Jacket oiled up. Pistol pants creased like razor blades. Even the black boots with the heel and toe taps were gleaming. It was curious, but in the confusion of Mel's ready confession, the cops had forgotten to confiscate the boots. You see, Mel was cool. Yeah, man, real cool.

He couldn't stop talking now. The stage was his. Had to play it neat all the way down the line. "Listen, man, I don't dig this mortuary, and I don't dig you! I don't dig no squares! This whole joint should be bopped! Just like the lame I iced! Yeah, man, this is too too crazy! I'd stack the whole bunch of you if I was the Big Man upstairs!"

What a beautiful noise his guys were making in the hallway. The judge's gavel banged again. The courtroom doors slammed open and closed and in a moment the cries from the corridor were muffled and dying away.

Court was recessed for two weeks to allow time for a psychiatric report on Mel. Would he kill again? A very distinct possibility for this existed, as he evinced no regard for human life, two state psychiatrists testified. Yet this lack of regard for life did not necessarily indicate insanity. The defendant was found to be grossly immature, but sane within the concept of the law. After several conferences in the judge's chambers, a court-appointed attorney decided against basing the defense on an insanity plea.

For the benefit of the record, the prosecutor made his necessary remarks in a professionally harsh and indignant delivery.

"Under the laws of our state, any person who causes the death of another person during the commission

149

of a felony, shall be deemed guilty of murder in the first degree. The defendant has admitted in open court that he was stealing a pair of boots from the deceased. He further admits to administering the beating which resulted in Mr. Steinberg's death. To some observers it may seem a bit harsh to invoke this particular law, thus automatically insuring the death penalty. Some people will also take issue with the idea of executing the defendant for what is obviously an unpremeditated crime. Others will protest because of the defendant's youth. Yet the other alternative is to simply charge the defendant with larceny, which carries a maximum penalty of four years.

"The display of savagery exhibited by Mel Warner is only one of a recent rash of similar killings that have been taking place in our city. It is our duty to clean the streets, to offer a deterrent against this violent upsurge. It is our obligation to protect the business people and the legitimate citizens of our community from this type of horror. The evidence presented here leaves no question of guilt or innocence. There remains only for you, the jury, to set the degree of this atrocity. I ask that you bring back a just verdict of guilty, and that the charge be murder one, and that there be no recommendation for mercy. The state will then exercise its duty, and there will be no fear of Mel Warner walking the streets of this city again. . . ."

Death Row is usually a quiet place. Mel didn't dig quiet places. He spent most of his time playing the latest rock 'n' roll, jazz and blues. Phonographs with headsets were the latest concessions to men waiting to die.

Eight men went to the chair during the sixty-day period Mel waited for his turn. Each time the lights dimmed, Mel shouted, "Go, man, go!" and put on another batch of platters.

He wasn't going for any soft, square routine. The

papers said he was a mean killer. A killer was supposed to be bad. He was real bad. Like the day he told off the sailor who had strangled the little girl in the park. Mel was irate with him for breaking into sobs when his time came.

"Get going, chump! You monsters never have any guts! Get going!"

Mel's attitude was the same toward Parker, the legal eagle who had managed to stave off his own execution for over six years.

"Give it up, clown! You can't outlast the hot-squat! Give it up!"

Parker simply smiled, adjusted his radio headphones, and kept on with his typing.

No one really paid Mel any mind. They heard, but they weren't really listening. The only way to show them how a *man* should go out, was by example. No copping deuces for him. No, he would not sign any papers for the governor! No, he did not want to see his mother! The priest could can his jazz, too. Yeah, okay, a short letter home to see that Lou Winters got his wheels. Yeah, man, Lou was a right stud.

The final meal was "out of sight." Mel's favorite dish: french fries, lettuce and tomato salad, two cheeseburgers deluxe, a quart of milk and five Coca-Colas. Very tasty.

The time had come. He was ready. "Okay, gang, I've got to cut out. Going to take the Edison Special! Yeah, man, the Edison Special!"

The inhabitants of Death Row remained silent.

"Cheer up, gang, cheer up! It'll be kicks! Yeah, that's it, real kicks!"

The priest tried again to talk to Mel. Was there anything he could do? A word for his mother? No, Mel wasn't diggin' it.

Mel's voice changed suddenly to a strange whisper, though still audible to everyone on Death Row. His tone was almost pathetic. "I'm just a kid, and I'm kinda scared."

Kindness and hope came into the priest's face. "How can I help, son?" he asked tenderly.

"Would you come along and hold my hand until it's over?"

The inmates of Death Row roared at the macabre joke. The priest's face reddened, then slowly lost all color. The warden and six guards entered the row. They had missed the joke.

"Are you ready, Warner?"

"Is a bluebird blue, Pop? I'm ready as I'll ever be."

"Any last thing you want to say? It's only a matter of minutes now."

Mel searched his mind frantically. He had to have something strong, something cool, something with impact. He had it.

"Yeah, Pop, if you're for real, there is one thing. I dig my black stomps the most."

The warden was for real. "Guard, bring the boy his boots."

NICOLE ROSALIE PAULZINE

Minnesota Correctional Institution for Women, Shakopee, Minnesota

This jazzy twenty-one-year-old fluff from "the land of ten thousand lakes" is the editor of her institutional paper, *The Reflector*. Niki has been interested in writing since she first started doing time at the tender age of fourteen. Her poetry reflects her feelings and has the effect of making one feel terribly bad or tearfully jubilant. She attributes this special sensitivity to the personalization factor, writing of and to the people she cares about most.

To My Parents

Niki Paulzine

i, your daughter, am all alone
behind walls—
steel bars—
unconscious cages—
strange facades—
While you, my parents
sit at home in your warm suburbia
at the foot of your color tv
   with all your tinsel, upstanding ways,
and self-righteous faces.
i, your daughter, am all alone
with my child, whom you call
none of yours—"illegitimate,"
unwanted, a child of sin.
While you, with my sister of twenty years,
(on your nineteenth wedding anniversary)
eat cake and drink a toast to 19 more,
i, your daughter, have sinned
exceedingly . . . forgotten your values,
thought for myself, made human mistakes,
While you, my pious examples
of perfection, lived confined in cages

of bigotous standards,
commit only white lies,
and think like the Joneses.
i, your daughter, am far from
perfect—i ran free in my youth,
tested my world . . . yet you,
my parents, won't allow me those
failures,
    the human mistakes,
        the lessons of learning.
i, your daughter, grew
in another age,
a day of awakening—
    when little girls weren't all
soft curls . . . they had intelligence
too . . . yet you, my parents,
won't accept my knowing,
   my straying from the
        kitchen and the woman's
predestined duty.
i, your daughter—your child of youth—
am all alone,
    in this world without you—
but i've retained my pride
(and my father's stubborn streak)
so i can't come without welcome to you.
i, your daughter—am trying to read,
or understand your ways & values;
but you, my parents,
refuse to allow me to apologize.
if i, your daughter, would come
to you and ask for a chance—
or just your friendship . . .
would you, my parents,
be humble enough to give me
that or slam the door
again?

i, your daughter—am growing
older, alone and weary,
bitter and sorry—i've developed new ways
of coping with problems
of escaping from life—from
    living and knowing.
i, your daughter—
am called
a junkie,
a derelict,
a doper,
a crook,
a creep,
a whore,
a hustler,
a killer,
a sinner,
yet i'm really your
lonely child.
Today, my parents, at dinner,
did you eat your steak, mashed potatoes and gravy,
smoke your tobacco, lean back and be grateful
for all your riches—or
did it cross your mind as
you passed the salt
how much i resembled your daughter
of twenty . . . and where i am at right now?
Did you, my parents, feel any remorse
or twinge of guilt, or ache
of loneliness—for your part in this
wrong situation?
Or did you erase all your capacity
for caring, of human life, of parental
instinct once and for all?
i, your daughter, am all alone—
cold, tired, slowly dying . . . rotting away
(inside where it hurts so bad) from all the pain

i'm bearing for my wrongs and yours.
i'm crumbling away—till all will be gone and i
am as worthless as you claim me to be.
i, your daughter, am asking for one more time—
please love me, or try to at least like me.
i'm really not rotten, or at least i'm human.
could you give me that much?
Could you, my parents, for once recognize me?
i am not of your time, i know not of your
standards, i can't accept your values . . . but i
have my own, and they're not all outlandish
or farfetched or stupid. Could you, my parents,
see me as i am, your daughter, your child, your
own?

Tree Outside My Window

Niki Paulzine

Outside my window you're growing
grasping out with gnarled arms
reaching for me
to rescue me from my plight.
your bony fingers
swathed in brown crispy wraps
seem to beg for me to meet them.
Are you some prince come to save me?
Time races on—
you seem even taller.
The seasons bring change
to your
stolid
somber
being.
In spring your green hues dance before my eyes
glazed with a frosting dew each morning
dazzling
like precious crystals in the dawn.
In summer—
you seem to thirst for relief
the green no longer fresh

rather parched
earthy.
In fall—
your bright autumn wardrobe flashes
the vibrant tones worthy only of a noble's dress.
Then winter—
before the first snow
you clutch your last tatters
now brown & gray & worn.
You hold fiercely to them
as I do my soul
only letting your fall array have its freedom
when at last the cold breaks your spirit
Another spring—
I watch the birds returning from the south
nestling in your arms
gaining shelter from the sun & rain.
Their babies serenade me
as their hungry mouths
continually beg for mothers' nourishment.
Outside my window
you're reaching for me
yet my arms are not quite long enough
to touch your fingers
and
my body is still locked away inside.
Perhaps another year
you'll grow another inch for me.
Will you reach for me again
next year
when at last I will be tall enough?
Will you set me free?

She Said

Niki Paulzine

She said, after years of waiting—
   i love you . . .
You are mine, of me, my daughter.
i wept tears not of sadness—
   but of joy!
She said in words unspoken—
   that she cared, and always had
but she never
   knew or grew enough
to speak. She touched—
reached out, from behind a wall
of pride and sorrow . . . that was
once impenetrable, and i too
allowed myself to touch
   from behind mine.
She said, after years of waiting,
i love you—and i cried.

JOSEPH MAXEY

Rahway State Prison, Rahway, New Jersey

Max is a prime example of the Blind Lady's justice. He came north from Richmond, Virginia, at the age of twenty, and up until that time hadn't garnered so much as a traffic ticket. In an effort to make friends, he ended up with a ghetto gang who one day jumped on a woman and assaulted her sexually. When the smoke cleared, Joe had double-life and all the weight! Fourteen years later he is still shaking his head in confusion, trying to figure out what he is doing in a place like this. No one is saying that people who commit crimes should go unpunished, but in this case there is a great deal of doubt, only not enough money to find out how much!

Trade-In

Joseph Maxey

As Emma slid into the front seat alongside Elton Brown, he took note of her skimpy white shorts and shook his head in exasperation. It wasn't that he was a prude, just that he felt some things should only be enjoyed by one man. He knew she was displeased, though, by the shorts and her hair, which she'd knotted up into a tight bun on the back of her head. It didn't make much difference if she was mad or not, since once he made a decision there wasn't any room for debate. She knew who was Mr. Top Cat. He often wondered, though, how it would be having her fly into a tirade or something, but he knew that she knew better than to try anything that foolish. He lifted the mike from the dashboard and spoke into the automatic driver control.

"Garton's Gardens."

The tired 1987 Colton Roadster digested the information, then with a meshing and whirring of gears, backed out of the driveway. Elton grimaced as the hoary machine groaned its way to cruising speed.

Fifteen minutes later the roadster turned into a long elm-shaded lane, coughed twice, and creaked to a halt in front of an oval-shaped structure the size of the Roman Colosseum. A ponderous revolving sign circled the top of the building, blinking in sequenced multicolored flashes: GARTON'S GARDENS YOU

    W   G   H   C   G

     O T E S O T H N E

      N'   T   R   A   D HERE

Emma climbed out without a word or waiting for Elton and walked briskly up the cobblestone path. She had to wait for him anyway, as the gilded frost-paned doors didn't open until he came up. An uncommonly thin salesman greeted Elton in the center of a luxuriously furnished reception room, took his hand and pumped it enthusiastically up and down.

"Good day, sir. Can I be of some help?"

"I'd like to browse a bit first," Elton said.

"Of course," the salesman said heartily, taking note of the last word Elton said, "first." "Things are slow right now, so I will accompany you myself." He threw a comradely arm around Elton's shoulders and ushered him into another room, a spacious affair, two hundred feet long and half as wide. Purple crepe drapes adorned the walls, flowing lazily in a synthetic man-made breeze, while schools of tropical fish scurried about beneath a transparent blue floor. The exhibits circling the room were awe-inspiring, each on its own little tropical island, surrounded by exotic shrubs and miniature palm trees.

"This is the lovely LT-4," the salesman said, stopping at the first display. "Gorgeous, isn't she? Look at those lines, those sweeping curves. . . . "

Elton admitted that the LT-4 was quite a sight, but he didn't intend to make any hasty decisions. "I'd like to see the others."

"Righto," the salesman bubbled, hiding his disappointment at not making a quick sale. "We have every size, type, color, make and model on the world market. We have imports from Europe, Asia, Africa, South America and Australia, every one tested and certified by the International Consumer Commission. I am positive we have something to suit your fancy, and your pocketbook. . . ."

Elton moved down the line to the next exhibit and the next, the next and the next. . . . An hour and a half later they were back in front of the LT-4. Elton still hadn't made up his mind. "How much for that one?"

The salesman tried to beam over his frustration, but it came off badly. "We're giving it away at six thousand."

"Six thousand credits is a lot of money," Elton said skeptically.

"You're getting a lot of machinery," the salesman countered. "The LT-4 is a model of perfection, precision-tuned by men dedicated to excellence. Our Detroit plant boasts the finest assembly line in the world. It's a gift at six thousand."

Elton wasn't sure. "I don't know. . . ."

The salesman pressed. "Think of the delight, the years of pure pleasure, the pride you'll feel at having the best money can buy." The thin merchant held up a hand for emphasis. "That isn't all . . . Garton's also includes a five-year warranty on all moving parts, plus for the first year you are automatically covered with a five-thousand-credit insurance policy. Now where else could you find a deal like that?"

Elton nodded, deciding to go for the LT-4. "Do you take trade-ins?"

The salesman grinned in earnest. It was about damn time! "Garton's takes anything tangible. Just last month we allowed five hundred credits on a mannequin. What year is your trade-in?"

"I bought her in '87."

"Whew!" the salesman exclaimed. "That's almost a collector's item." He looked out toward the reception room, where he saw Emma staring dejectedly through the frost-paned door at the old Colton Roadster. "She looks good from here."

"She is," Elton said, surprised to feel the stirrings of remorse.

The salesman pursed his lips thoughtfully. "Give you six hundred for her," he said presently.

Elton stared at him incredulously. "I paid eight thousand!"

"Nine hundred is tops," the salesman quipped quickly, "and that's because I like you."

Elton shook his head. "No," he said firmly.

The salesman frowned. "Let's see what we're getting here," he said, and walked out into the reception room.

Emma started when the salesman came up behind her, but recovered quickly and stood motionless while he examined her, sparing not even the most intimate parts. Elton had to look away.

"Twenty-three years old, you say," the salesman said appreciatively, straightening up. "I'll let you have fifteen hundred."

Elton ventured a guilty glance at Emma, turning goggle-eyed when he saw the quivering lips and the tears rolling down her pale cheeks. The salesman noticed too and was impressed. Detroit was still in the experimental stage on this.

"That's a sweet job of customizing there," the salesman said. "She sure looks convincing. How'd you manage it? It mean, dolls and these things just aren't the same. Water gets into the electrical circuit and poof. . . . Damn Safety Council won't allow it. . . . What'd you do?"

Elton's confusion was obvious. "I . . . I . . . I . . . didn't do anything!"

The salesman recognized craftiness when he saw it.

168

He thought of the money to be made on a patented sprinkler system that worked safely. "Come on, robots don't just start crying by themselves. You had to make some additions."

"I told you," Elton said evenly, "I didn't do anything."

The salesman made as if to touch Emma again, but this time Elton's harsh voice arrested him. "Keep your damn hands off her!"

The salesman scowled. Something funny was going on here, and he wanted to know what it was. "I'll give you the LT-4 even up."

Elton ignored him, thought back to the time he came down with the Asian flu, the way Emma remained at his bedside, wiping his forehead, feeding him hot broth, climbing in beside him at night and warming him with her own body. He remembered their trip to the mountains last year and the way she sat silently at his side while he fished, just being there. He thought of the home she kept spotless, the way she moved about the kitchen singing as she prepared his daily meals. The memories troubled him, yet made him want to jump for joy because somewhere, somehow a machine had taken on the feelings and emotions of a woman. He didn't know where Detroit messed up, but right now he didn't care. No damn machine could make strawberry dumplings like that! Robot, hell!

The salesman continued to babble. "The LT-4 and five thousand. Not another dime."

Elton wasn't even listening. He did glance at the beautiful LT-4, standing ghostlike just inside the showroom doorway. All over the world factories were turning out assembly-line models like her, replicas of human beings, supposedly without human faults or feelings. Mankind had become so proficient at duplicating human hair, skin, even some internal organs, that it was nearly impossible to tell the difference. Perhaps they had gone too far.

"I think you people better wake up," Elton said, knowing that his words fell on deaf ears.

"What are you cackling about?" the salesman growled, seeing no further reason to butter Elton up.

Elton grinned rougishly at Emma and offered her his arm. She'd removed the pins from her hair and as she shook it out around her shoulders, she laughed, a warm tinkling sound. Then came more tears, but these were of a different kind and Elton didn't care if she cried like that forever.

"Let's go, woman," he chuckled. "Might as well start getting used to you giving me trouble. . ."

Behind the retreating couple and the salesman, the LT-4 moved a hand across her moistened eyes, but slowly, so that she wouldn't be detected. A moment later the old Colton Roadster roared off and the shallow little salesman spun angrily on his heel. Before he completed his turn, the LT-4 had her best Detroit smile back in place.

PAUL M. FITZSIMMONS

Trenton State Prison, Trenton, New Jersey

Fitz, a graduate of The Famous Writers' School, has been at it for almost fifteen years. After reading some of his efforts, one can't help being amazed that such a talent hasn't gained a foothold in today's wide-open literary market. His earlier contributions to our first volume, *Voices from the Big House,* brought him praise from all parts of the country, so we didn't hesitate to scoop up "Did I Do That, Really?" for these pages.

Did I Do That, Really?

Paul M. Fitzsimmons

When the subdued but insistent tinkle of the phone rang in her blue-wallpapered bedroom, Cissie was on her bed, an exposé magazine in her hand and a bored expression clouding her pretty, high-cheekboned face. In addition to this expression of boredom, she wore only the tops of a pink set of shorty pyjamas and a pair of white panties, so sheer and unsubstantial as to have been spun of cigarette smoke.

She let the blue princess phone ring a few more times, until the persistent clatter gave a short moment of aggravation, then she languidly put the receiver to her ear. Her firmly rounded breasts rose heavily with the motion of her arm.

"Hello," she murmured into the mouthpiece.

"Hello, baby," came a low voice.

"Who's this?" Cissie wanted to know.

"Take a guess," the voice said.

"Well, you do sound kind of familiar. Have I been out with you before?"

"Not exactly, but we are pretty well acquainted."

Cissie crossed one slender and smoothly tanned leg

over the other and waggled her metallically painted toenails at the ceiling. "Hmm, I don't know whether or not I like the way you said that. Just *how well* are we acquainted?"

"Well, baby cakes, I'll put it this way—we're as close as man and woman can get, without getting married."

"Oh . . . I see . . . I see. . . ."

"Know who I am now?"

"Well . . . maybe if you told me what you look like it would be easier."

"Okay . . . let's see, I'm tall, a little on the skinny side, twenty-five years old, unmarried and simply crazy about cute blondes, who are so easy to get strung out on. Does that ring any bells?"

"Mmmmmmmmm. Tall, bony and oversexed, huh? Well, let me see. . . . Could you be Mike Skinner?"

"Nope, this isn't Mike Skinner."

"Uh . . . Bob Fennelly?"

"Nope."

"I got it! You're Pete McGuire."

"Bad guess."

"Ah, yes . . . You're Glen Thomas, I should . . ."

"Wrong again, baby. I'm not Glen Thomas and your ESP certainly isn't working tonight. Sure does deflate a guy's ego. . . ."

"Damn! Well, then . . . tell me where we met and maybe I can figure it from there."

"It was at a party."

"That's no help, dummy. I meet everybody at parties. What kind of party, silly?"

"As a matter of fact, it was a lousy bash until this certain little blonde made the scene."

"Yeah, and I bet that blonde was . . ."

"Absolutely correct, baby, li'l ole you."

Cissie frowned prettily and stared thoughtfully at her reflection in a mirror over the dressing table. "Just

174

what did I do at this blast to create such a sensation?"

"Oh, but baby, what didn't you do! Wowee! Did you ever let your hair down!"

"Soooo," Cissie said, her voice a half octave lower, "what did I do?"

"You mean you honestly don't remember?" The voice at the other end of the line sounded incredulous. "Baby, have you got a lousy memory, or a convenient one?"

"Look, just what do you mean by that crack? Was I drinking vodka at this shindig? Man, whenever I drink that stuff! I bet that's what I was drinking, huh?"

"Baby, you were drinking everything but lighter fluid. You were kinda slow getting started, but once you got cranked up, you were something else, especially after you started that little dance of yours."

"What dance? What's wrong with dancing? I mean, everybody dances, don't they?"

"Yeah, sure they do, but not like that! I mean, it wasn't the fact that you were dancing, it was the *way* you were dancing—and when you took off your blouse, I almost blew my mind!"

"What's so bad about that? I've been to parties where everything. . . ."

"I'll bet you have, baby, but you didn't have no bra on and you do bounce around so nicely."

"Okay, okay, already. . . . So what happened then?"

"Then? Then you took off your mini and just like on top, there wasn't anything else to take off."

"Oh, good God! Don't tell me I did that again?"

"You sure did, honey, and much more, bumping and grinding better than any stripper I've ever seen, and they make their living doing it. Anyway, the result was out of sight!"

"Oh, man! That's the first time I ever went that far . . . I think . . . I mean . . . I hope it was. Well,

175

tell me the rest of the sordid details, as if you didn't plan to anyway."

"Well, after you almost blew everybody's mind, you laid down on the sofa and all the fellows. . . ."

"Wait one damn minute! Now just wait a minute! How many were there?"

"Hmm, about half a dozen, I'd guess. Anyway, all the fellows. . . ."

"No!" Cissie broke in indignantly. "Stop! I don't believe none of it! I have never . . . well, once I let two fellows take me out and we did sort of make the scene, but except for that one time . . . I have never in my life. . . . half a dozen, humph!"

"Just calm down, sugar. Calm down and let me finish. I was getting ready to say that all the fellows figured maybe you should lie down for a while in one of the bedrooms, until you were feeling better. So, I sort of took you in hand, ha-ha, and carried you into the bedroom. . . ."

"Yeah, oh yeah, and all these other guys didn't do anything but stand around and look, huh? I'll just bet they did."

"Sure they stared. Who wouldn't? But that's all. I swear it."

"Humph. Then the whole bunch must have been sick or something. So, you put me to bed and then you sat around playing pinochle until I came to again, huh?"

"No . . . not exactly that, baby. When I got you in the bedroom you sort of, you know, you had quite a load on and you started fooling around with me and . . ."

"Yes, and you took advantage of me, huh? Why, you should be ashamed of yourself, taking advantage of a defenseless girl who had a little too much to drink. You really should be ashamed of yourself!"

"Hold on, baby, back up a minute. You got this all bass-ackwards. You took advantage of *me!* I mean, I actually tried to get out of the room so I wouldn't take advantage of you, but you kept grabbing me and wiggling around on the bed . . . I just couldn't take it."

Cissie giggled suddenly. "I did? Really? Then what happened?"

"Well . . . then you sort of, kind of . . . I mean you pulled me down on the bed with you."

Cissie giggled again. "I bet you struggled damn hard, too, trying to get away from me."

"No, I didn't struggle at all. I'm only human and you're a very beautiful and sexy woman. You weren't playing either. The slacks I had on that night are down at the tailor's now, having a new. . . ."

"Okay! Okay! I believe you . . . I believe you. Man, what that vodka makes me do! So, continue, man. . . ."

"What do you think happened next, baby?"

"Yes. Yes. I know, but," Cissie's voice dropped to a soft, throaty murmur, "*how* did it happen?"

"Well, if you don't remember that, I don't know if it's right to tell you. I mean. . . ."

"Oh, come off the soapbox! You simply must tell me what took place." Cissie wiggled her voluptuous hips against the sheets, then flopped over onto her belly, her large breasts pushed in by the pillow, their nipples hardening in memory, or was it anticipation? She pressed the receiver closer to her ear, not wanting to miss one little detail.

"Please," she begged, "please tell me what we did, everything."

"I got a better idea, since I'm in the neighborhood. How about if I . . . you know, dropped over for a visit and we can have a rerun? I'm real close by."

"I don't know about that." Cissie smiled to herself, rolled over and laid her tousled blonde head against the pillow. Her bottom squirmed sinuously. "I was

177

just going to take a hot bath and then set my hair, you know, go to bed early for a change."

"Well, you still can, sugar. I won't get in the way."

"Hmmm . . . I don't know. . . ."

"Tell you what. I'll even bring some vodka. How's that?"

Cissie's breasts lifted and thrust against the flimsy nightshirt. "Well . . . okay . . . but only for a little while. . . ."

"Hey, I hear you, Kathy! I'll grab the vodka and be right. . . ."

"What?" Cissie sat straight up in the bed. "What did you just call me?"

"Huh?"

"Dummy. I said, what did you just call me? It sounded very much like *Kathy*."

"It *was* Kathy. That's your name, isn't it? Don't you remember me yet? We met at Billy Thorpe's party last Tuesday. I'm Chuck Stevens. I knew you were loaded, but I didn't think you were that bombed out."

"But nothing! You listen to me! I don't know any Chuck Stevens or a Billy Thorpe! Furthermore, my name is not Kathy!"

"Aren't you kinda short, with big blue eyes and a lot of freckles on your. . . ."

"I am not short, and I do not have one freckle! You got the wrong number, Buster!"

"Isn't this SKyview 5-4828?"

"It certainly is not! This is SHoreline 5-8482, and boy, are you ever a bungler! Well, you blew this one!"

"Wait . . . even if your name isn't Kathy, I mean, we have sort of gotten acquainted . . . I still could get a bottle and drop over. After all. . . ."

"Drop dead, creep!" Cissie shouted into the phone. "What kind of a girl do you think I am?"

WHAMMMMMMMMMMMM, went the receiver.

Cissie rolled onto her belly again, crossed her forearms over her breasts and let out a gust of air. "Boy oh boy!" she snorted angrily to herself, before picking up the exposé magazine again. "That Kathy must be some kind of tramp!"

LARRY (SHADE) OGBURN

Rahway State Prison, Rahway, New Jersey

Shade comes out of Newark, New Jersey.
He is twenty-five years old and has been
"down" eight years. He arrived at the prison
when he was only seventeen, toting a sixty-
year load, and during the ensuing time
has matured into a serious young man. He
devotes most of his time to writing essays
and has been published in *Fortune News*
and *African Voice*. His aim now is, aside
from maintaining some semblance of sanity
in this madhouse, to get a taste of freedom,
while it is still out there to get.

Would You Be Normal?

Larry Ogburn

Hey, you! On the bus, on the corner, in that house, riding in that car, sitting at that desk, making love to that woman, playing with those beautiful children, looking at that damn TV. Hey! Listen to me, I got something to ask you.

Would you be normal if all you saw for eight years were bars, steel, and hundreds of meshed-wire reinforced doors, which are there to keep you inside a vicious, savage compound?

Would you be normal if every day all you saw and were subservient to were guards who are illiterate, gung-ho, Gestapo-minded perpetrators of your subjugation?

Would you be normal if you lost your wife, mother, son, father and brothers because you were in prison serving a sixty (60)-year sentence?

Would you be normal while being forcibly confined to and contained in an area the size of a freshly dug grave, "7x6x5," as year after year of your allotted existence rushed by because there is nothing you can do but wait to die?

Would you be normal while walking around in circles

183

in a compound yard, seeing and knowing that at all times you are walking with several 30/30 automatic rifles and pump shotguns hovering on the wall to blow your brains out?

Would you be normal after working for slave wages (45¢ per day) and on top of that, knowing that the jobs you hold in prison don't even exist on the outside?

Would you be normal if your father died while you were in this cesspool from an incompetent nurse's breaking a damn needle off in him, causing his death, and you were denied the right to attend his funeral because neither you nor the rest of your family had the required forty-two dollars which is demanded by the institution to pay for the use of two guards and a car for that day?

Would you be normal if your keeper pugnaciously and systematically conditioned you to believe that you were foul, scum, a demented savage, who was unfit to be among other people?

Tell me the truth! Would you be normal when everything around you functions to negate your normality?

The above being the facts of the matter, your response must be negative, and in accordance with that, I beg you to tell me why you demand that my actions be in accord with normalcy after I've been subjected for eight years to sadistically perpetrated abnormality?

Am I not a human being just like you? Am I not a person with *feelings,* who laughs, cries, lives and dies just like you?

THINK! I was seventeen (17) years old when I was shipped off to prison; accused, indicted, convicted and sentenced to 60 years! Yes, you people who are *just like me* killed that seventeen-year-old boy. He is dead forever . . . and now . . . YOU ARE KILLING THE MAN! Will you tell me why he too must die?

RON GREENFIELD

Virginia State Penitentiary, Richmond, Virginia

I Wish I Were a Unicorn

Ron Greenfield

Not too many people are familiar with unicorns, but I happen to be an expert on them.

A long time ago, when I was much younger, I met this old unicorn and at first I was really scared because I had thought that unicorns didn't exist. Now that I am older, I know different. Anyway, this unicorn told me a little about himself.

First off, when he was growing up there were two divisions among the unicorns; those with shiny horns called "bips," and those with dull horns called "bops." Now the bops had to do all the hunting and cleaning, while the bips did nothing but lay around and think of how to make the bops work harder. But one day the leader of the unicorns (who was a bip) decided that if both groups worked together they would both make out much better. "After all," he said, "whether you're a bip or a bop, you're still a unicorn, and if we don't care about each other, who will?"

So the bips and the bops started to work and play together, and pretty soon there were no bips or bops, just unicorns, who grew more and more happy. They would help each other out, and as quiet as it is kept, the unicorns would go to the riverside and eat that wacky weed and get high together.

All in all, things were going very smoothly, till one day the world started to close in on the unicorns. Everywhere they looked there was hate and mistrust, so the unicorns packed up their belongings and moved to a place where no one could find them, and they won't ever come out until the world learns what the unicorns did. . . .

I looked at this old unicorn telling me the story, and noticed that he had a big tear in his eye. Being young and foolish, I asked him what the matter was, and he said that one day I'd know. Then he turned his tail and ran off.

I often think of this old unicorn now and then, and wonder when we will ever learn. I don't have the answer, and I don't think the unicorns even know.

WILLIAM McCURRY

New Mexico State Penitentiary, Santa Fe, New Mexico

Another Christmas Carol

William McCurry

E. S. Kruge didn't like Christmas. It wasn't anything personal. E. S. Kruge also didn't like Columbus Day, Memorial Day, the Fourth of July, or any of the other holidays that cluttered the calendar. When houses of business closed, Kruge was forced to suspend his operations and he didn't like this, because the driving passion in his life was his tireless and successful pursuit of the dollar. It was this attitude, coupled with the date, December 23rd, that accounted for the stormy expression clouding his countenance as he strode purposefully into the conference room.

With a curt nod of acknowledgment to the men and women already assembled, Kruge tossed his briefcase on the polished top of the long table and, with a flip of his hand, cut off the voices raised in greeting.

"Let's knock off the courtesies," he snapped, "and get on with it!"

He motioned with the flat of his hand, and everyone immediately sat. It was a gift Kruge possessed. Instant compliance. It had long ceased to surprise him. He let his hard, sharp eyes sweep over the assemblage as they watched him, trying to size him up. He knew what they saw: a lean, distinguished man in his early fifties, a man with the menacing air of an enraged cobra. That was the impression he tried to give. That was the impression he gave.

"I'm E.S. Kruge," he said.

They nodded.

"I'm the new boss," he said.

They nodded again.

"Of some of you!"

They stared.

"Some of you will not want to work for me," he explained. And with lips formed into a cold, thin smile, he continued, "And some of you can't work for me." Tact! Diplomacy! The Kruge trademark.

"The former chairman of the board . . . and also majority stockholder of this company, started out in business with me many years ago. When he died last week," and there was no hint of sorrow in Kruge's voice, "I became owner of all his holdings." He paused to observe their reactions.

"If I had gone first," he continued, "he—Jake Marlow—would have taken over my interests. It was our original agreement."

Flipping open his briefcase, he began to thumb through the papers it contained. Without looking up, he resumed his monologue. "I'm not telling you all of this because it's any of your business. It's not!" he looked up from under his brows. "I'm telling you because I want you to understand that I did not get this business through love or charity, and," his look became more menacing, "it won't be run on either of those weaknesses."

Lifting a document, Kruge examined it briefly, then snapped, "Which one of you is Crockett?"

A hand went up on Kruge's left. "That's me," said the man. Kruge examined him. Lean . . . late thirties . . . with the look of stubborn persistence about him.

"All right, Crockett, what's this?" He looked down at the paper he held. "What's this Devil's Horn project? It appears to be the largest impending venture, and you seem to figure in it heavily."

As Kruge waited expectantly, Crockett rose and walked to a map hanging on the near wall. Average height, self-confident; like a computer, Kruge filed away details of everyone he dealt with.

"Right here," said Crockett, slowly tapping a spot on the map. "Right here is a peak called Devil's Horn. It's a . . ."

"I know *where* it is," Kruge interrupted, "and I know *what* it is. I want to know *why*." He looked genuinely puzzled for a moment. "I want to know why a good, sharp businessman like Jake Marlow would even have considered investing money in some harebrained scheme to build a giant ski complex and," he paused to glance at the papers he held, "an Alpine village." He almost sneered. "And all of it practically on the edge of the desert!" He thumped the table. "Why?"

Crockett glanced briefly at the others, then met Kruge's challenging gaze. "Mr. Kruge," he started, "many of us came over to Marlow Enterprises only because of the Devil's Horn project. That includes me."

"So?" asked Kruge.

"We—that is, I—think it's a solid and sound project." He shrugged, as though his explanation was sufficient.

"Convince me!" Kruge snapped. "Make it brief and make it concise, but convince me." It was a dare.

Crockett eyed him levelly for a moment. "All right. . . . One—magnificent scenery. Two—potentially unparalleled ski runs. Three—it'll be the closest luxury complex to the southwestern population centers. Four—" he paused, "four—enormous profit potential. Added to all of that, it can fill a need in the recreational field and help local economy, and—well, love, I guess. That is also a part of it."

The barest trace of a smile had started to move Kruge's hard mouth, but the last few words froze him. "Love!" he snarled. "Well, now, why don't we just take our money and drop it over this—this Devil's Horn. That would sure help the economy." He shook his head. "I'm sure they'd love that."

A pink tinge flushed Crockett's features and he kept his eyes lowered as he replied. "The love I meant was our—or at least, my—love of the big country, the clean air and the winter sports." He hesitated, as though gathering his nerve, then went on. "But most of all, those people out there." He waved a hand toward the map. "Those people had faith in Jake Marlow—enough faith to buy lots and building sites. Some even hinged their entire futures on his promise of what would be done."

He placed his hands on the table and leaned toward Kruge. "It's their money, Mr. Kruge, their investment money that Jake Marlow used to help buy up those hills. And it's those people who'll be left with worthless land in a deserted area if the project isn't carried through."

Kruge's face had remained immobile during Crockett's speech. When he finally did speak, his voice was chilled with icy sarcasm. "How touching! How noble! How stupid!" Again his fist thudded against the table. "Profit!" he thundered. "Profit, Crockett! Nothing matters but profit. Those people can all go to the—Devil's Horn, for all I care."

Kruge walked to a large window behind the table and stood for a moment surveying the city that sprawled below. "And I think I might just be able to salvage a profit," he said, as though to himself. He wheeled around and moved back to the table. "Yes, I think I just might be able to make a profit out of it yet." He looked directly at Crockett. "And it won't be from building some ski-bum haven, either."

194

Crockett came halfway out of his seat, but Kruge held up that imperious hand. "Oh, I'll talk to these noble people of yours. But just remember what I'm after. Money! Loot! Profit!" His eyes gleamed. "That's what does the persuading with E.S. Kruge." He sat down. "Now, everyone out! Everyone except you, Crockett."

He waved his hand, and again the magic obedience was the result. Everyone rose, like well-behaved sheep, and started for the door without a word of protest. Except Crockett, who said, "Just a moment. They have an interest in Devil's Horn too. They should hear whatever plans you have."

"I'm sure you'll fill them in adequately," Kruge sneered. "Then again, there just might not be any plans, or any Devil's Horn."

Crockett sank back into his chair, silent until the door closed and they were alone.

"Crockett," said Kruge, "you have a good résumé, and you know the full workings of this thing. . . ." Crockett wanted to say something, but Kruge waved him impatiently off. "Colorado is loaded with fancy winter resorts, and even New Mexico has the nucleus of one." He got to his feet. "We'll leave in the morning, Crockett. You and me, we'll fly to your Devil's Horn and we'll. . . ." He trailed off at the look of consternation on Crockett's face. "Is something wrong?" he asked.

"Tomorrow is Christmas Eve," Crockett said. "My oldest boy is in the Marine Corps, and he'll be home for the first time in. . . ."

"So you'll miss Christmas with him," Kruge said offhandedly. "You can take him out for New Year's. We'll be back by then."

Crockett looked pained. "It's just not the same. Christmas has always been sort of special to us. I'd rather wait until after Christmas, if you don't mind."

195

"I *do* mind," Kruge said frostily. "I mind very much! I will assume your refusal to accompany me constitutes your resignation, and act accordingly." While he talked, he peeled the foil from one of his custom cigars. "Is that it?" he asked, peering up from beneath lowered brows and applying flame to the cigar.

Crockett, after a slight pause, sighed wearily. "Mr. Kruge, if it wasn't nearly Christmas and if this project wasn't so important, I'd tell you what to do with your assumption. But," he shrugged, "I'll go." He stood up.

Kruge nodded and also rose. "Yes, I thought you would." He started putting papers into his briefcase. "Be at my hangar in the morning, six o'clock sharp. Southwest Air Terminal."

Crockett, head tilted slightly, studied Kruge for a moment. "They just about pinned the tail on the donkey when they named you, didn't they?"

"Donkey?" asked Kruge. "Name?"

"Scrooge," said Crockett. "It should have been Scrooge."

Crockett left, but his jibe had been wasted. Kruge was immune to insults.

The office used by Kruge's former partner, J.J. Marlow, was on the floor above the conference room. Kruge sat behind the massive walnut desk, looking around at the impressive decor, thinking how the years had evidently changed Marlow. The furnishings spoke of quiet, cultured taste. Not the old Marlow at all.

"You were making it, Jake, old boy," he mused aloud. "Only that soft streak stopped you from being a giant, but in a few months I'll have this outfit on a level with my own. Who knows? I may end up owning the whole country." He chuckled.

The buzzer on the intercom interrupted his soliloquy. "Yes," he said, flipping the switch.

"Telephone, sir," said a metallic voice, "on line three."

Kruge's practiced eye quickly scanned the buttons in front of him. He flipped the correct one and said, "Kruge here."

The answering voice belonged to his nephew, Sumner. "Uncle Eb? Sumner here. Thought I'd call and offer my congratulations on your takeover of Marlow's outfit."

"Humph!" snorted Kruge. "Anything else?"

"Well, yes. . . . Sue and I wondered if you might be able to come over for Christmas. We're having a few . . ."

"Christmas Smistmas," sneered Kruge. "Christmas? Just another working day. I'll not waste my time with Christmas, just because a lot of wage leeches want to steal time from their employers."

"Well," drawled his nephew slowly, as though he wanted to say something else. "Okay, Uncle Eb. Maybe another time. Congratulations again." The line went softly dead.

Kruge spent the remainder of the day dictating memoranda that established new policies and efficiently taking care of all the most pressing correspondence. When he finally did decide to leave the office, his secretary looked up.

"Good-bye, Mr. Kruge," she smiled, "and Merry Christmas!"

Kruge stopped and slowly turned. Then, looking the girl directly in the eye, he said loudly and distinctly, "Bah! Humbug!"

It was shortly before noon the next day when the sleek Learjet nosed down to survey the landing strip below Devil's Horn. The single runway had been cleared of snow as the result of a phone call from Bob Crockett the day before. Crockett thought of the hurried labor involved, but considered it likely that Kruge took it as a matter of course.

Kirby Ross, Kruge's pilot, had his hands full in managing the swift jet within the narrow confines of the steep mountains that surrounded the landing strip, but with precise skill he floated the plane expertly to the ground, bringing it to a soft stop near the end of the runway.

Kruge, though hard and apparently lacking in compassion, was not immune to beauty. In fact, he had acquired a cultured taste and a keen sense of appreciation for those things beautiful, and as the men alighted from the aircraft, Kruge took in the awe-inspiring magnificence.

There was no town, only a few scattered shacks clustered around a large pre-fabricated airplane hangar. The relatively flat meadow, which had afforded the room to carve out the airstrip, was completely surrounded by steep slopes just bristling with snow-covered evergreens. In many places jagged rocks added eye-pleasing ruggedness to the lovely landscape, while on one side of the valley, rocky cliffs exposed multi-hued stone for hundreds of feet. Across the entire horizon, snow-capped peaks thrust sharp fingers skyward, and over it all loomed the Devil's Horn.

To Kruge the peak was slightly reminiscent of the Matterhorn, but more striking, more menacing, with its sharp tip curving outward as it narrowed to a point. It actually looked like some animal's horn—or devil's horn.

A small group of men waited, so Kruge and Crockett moved forward to meet them.

"Gentlemen," said Crockett, "meet E.S. Kruge."

Kruge gave a short nod, then shook hands with each man briefly as he was introduced by name.

Anders—outdoorsy, big, quick-moving, hard and intelligent eyes.

Davenport—pudgy, overly friendly, perhaps a guise to throw one off balance. Caution! Might be very shrewd.

Click! Click! Click! As the name was said, Kruge filed it away, along with whatever data his eyes or intuition could pick up.

Cook. Salman. Cartier. Kruge filed them all.

"All right, gentlemen," he said, "let's get on with our business."

Davenport emerged as the group spokesman. "We talked to Crockett last night, so I think we know your feelings. I also think we have what you want." He motioned toward the nearest shack. "If you'll join us over here, we can get started."

Inside the hut—it was hardly more—Davenport gave Kruge the information he felt was pertinent. All parties involved were experienced businessmen with something to offer a winter resort. True, the resort would be off the beaten path, but that was one of its assets. There would be no roads into the area and air-taxi service would be run from the major population centers. The town would be a reproduction of an Alpine village before the turn of the century. As they talked, the picture emerged as a sort of winter Disneyland. Kruge nodded at the conclusion.

"Only one thing wrong," he said, spreading his hands on the table and saying nothing more. Davenport finally broke the silence.

"What one thing?"

"No roads means no cars, means no people!" Kruge said.

Davenport shook his head in disagreement. "But we told you—air-taxi service!"

Kruge waved it off. "Might bring in a few. Not enough."

Crockett spoke up. "Mr. Kruge, a winter resort isn't like Coney Island, or a bowling alley. People don't

199

come to a luxury ski resort for an hour or two! They come for a weekend, two weeks, a month, some even longer! They come to escape the everyday bustle of the outside world, if only for a little while. No roads will mean no cars, no noise, no pollution and that's what they'll be coming here for, escape, respite, a chance to catch their breaths before digging back in and facing the everyday chore of living."

Kruge looked at Crockett skeptically. "I'll consider that idea." He turned to Davenport. "I assume you have some sort of transportation that will permit me to tour the area?"

Davenport nodded. "Yes, if you know how to use a snowmobile."

Kruge allowed himself a thin smile. "You would be surprised at just what I can manage. All right, trot it out! I want to take a good look at some of those fantastic ski runs you have mapped out." He waved a hand at the diagrams pinned to a wall.

"Fine," said Davenport. "One of us will go with you."

"None of you will go with me!" said Kruge. "I want to look things over alone, in my own way, in my own time, without a whole lot of babbling in my ear!"

The machine was one of the better snowmobiles, and it climbed the steep slopes with ease. As Kruge sped up and down hills, he was forced to admit that the location would make a great ski area. If only it wasn't situated in the middle of nowhere!

Kruge turned the little machine upward and kept climbing, until the evergreens thinned out completely and he was above the timberline. At one particular summit he stopped and looked down at the miniscule world below, thousands of feet down. The view was incomparable, surpassing anything Kruge had ever seen before, and he thought he had seen it all. For an instant, a very short instant, he felt almost insignificant.

"Humph!" he snorted. He felt a sudden chill and glanced at his watch, surprised to see how much time had elapsed. He glanced up and saw the sun dipping below the Devil's Horn. The peak was magnificent, but instead of its former inspiring appearance, it now seemed threatening, personally threatening. He shivered involuntarily and turned to mount the snowmobile.

Light snowflakes began to whip toward him, as he started carefully down the steep incline. "Funny," he thought at the suddenly darkened sky, "it wasn't cloudy a few moments ago." Kruge and the machine sped down the mountain much faster now.

The clouds continued to build, rapidly, darkly. The snow became thicker and the wind grew in force. Kruge had never known panic, but now the tiny fingers of apprehension raced up and down the entire length of his body.

Suddenly, through the rushing snow, Kruge saw a huge form materialize in front of his machine. He twisted the handle bars frantically, but too late—and the snowmobile smashed solidly into a giant granite boulder.

Kruge went over the handle bars, as the snowmobile writhed off to the side like a wounded animal, balanced precariously for a long second, then tumbled slowly over the edge of a precipice that hadn't been visible before. Kruge's inert form lay at the base of the boulder, still and unmoving.

The snow increased in velocity. The wind built to a shriek. What little sunlight had penetrated the clouds disappeared and gave way to the night. The temperature dropped, lower and lower. Over it, unseen, hung the Devil's Horn.

It was much later when Kruge gave the first indication that he was still alive. He moaned softly, stirred, then rolled slowly onto his back. As memory returned he squeezed his eyes tightly shut. He could have

201

sworn . . . no! It couldn't have been! But for a split second before he had hit the boulder, he was sure he had seen Jake Marlow standing in the snow. Slowly, reluctantly, he opened his eyes and looked around. All he saw was the wall of snowflakes falling on and around him. Of course! No Marlow, no nothing! What was it Scrooge had said? Oh yes, "an undigested bit of porridge." No, that wasn't it, but something like it.

Slowly, feeling his way, Kruge crawled up close to the face of the boulder that had wrecked his snowmobile, seeking its little shelter. Now to take stock, think things out, seek a solution to his present dilemma. It wasn't wise to move much. He had noted the sheer drop-off that had claimed the machine just before he had lost consciousness. "No," he said aloud. "Better stay right here. Wait it out. If I can last that long," he added wryly.

He leaned his head against the rock and closed his eyes. The cold was intense, penetrating even the thick quilted jacket he wore. He felt himself becoming lethargic. He dozed.

He woke with a start. Something had brushed his cheek! Something other than the snow! He opened his eyes, and shut them quickly again.

"Oh no! Not that!" But standing in front of him, close enough to touch, was a bright, shiny figure.

"You . . . you're . . . you can't be!"

"I am," the figure said gently. "I'm Christmas Past. Now grab hold and let's get going."

Kruge shook his head in disbelief and frustration. "This is absurd! You don't exist! You're just some fairy-tale creature, conjured up by my battered head." He squeezed his eyes shut. "Go away."

"Come on, now," said the figure pleasantly. "You know what we must do. You've read your Dickens." The bright face smiled politely and after Kruge opened his eyes, he had the overpowering feeling that the apparition was indeed real, though he knew better.

"Oh, all right!" he groaned. "I'll just dream this on out."

He reached out to touch the figure and experienced a wild, whirling sensation. Suddenly the snow disappeared and he was no longer on the snow-covered mountain in the midst of a snarling blizzard. Instead, in front of him stretched a grass-covered meadow and in the distance a house. His house! Or at least the house he lived in when he was a boy.

He forced himself to relax, knowing it was only a dream, and settled back to watch. It was odd though, like seeing a CinemaScope version of his life, and in living color too.

As his escort took him back through the years, Kruge remarked more than once on the similarity between his life and that of the fabled Ebenezer Scrooge.

His tour guide agreed.

Old Kruge did feel a pang of remorse, when he watched young Kruge break up with his girl, but only for a moment. "She was a fine girl," he told his guide. "Sweet, gentle Shirley. You know what? I'd like to see her again."

The shining face smiled, bowed slightly, and began to fade from sight.

"Wait!" Kruge shouted, and was immediately embarrassed. "Okay," he whispered. "It's just a dream. Bring on Christmas Present and Christmas Future."

And they came. Separately.

The trips were not pleasant—not a bit—and Kruge wished they would stick to the original version. It was much too personal, with himself as the star. He didn't like seeing what others thought of him, even if it was a dream of his own making.

Finally it ended and he found himself on the mountain. Alone. He dozed again.

Perhaps it was the cold or perhaps the shrieking wind that roused Kruge from his reverie, but he opened his eyes almost gratefully and huddled against the bare rock. He thought back over the past, remembering the things he had just dreamed. "Most upsetting!" he told himself. "I can almost see why old Scrooge reformed. No! No remorse. Not for me. Not for E.S. Kruge. Only an idiot would let a dream or childhood memories from a Christmas story change him. But I won't. Not me! Still . . . but what does it matter? I'd be a fool to think I'll ever get down off of this mountain. . . . A few more hours of exposure and that'll be the end of E.S. Kruge. And who will inherit? Probably Sumner, my fool nephew! And that wife of his, Sue. Let me see now . . . do they have two kids . . . or three? Not really bad youngsters. No, not at all. As a matter of fact, they've all been pretty nice to a hard-bitten old man like myself. And Sue . . . well, she's always gone out of her way to please me. Maybe, just maybe, if I can get off this confounded mountain, we might . . . oh no! None of that! I'm not going to ever get down off this mountain. Old Devil's Horn has got me for sure! But why the Devil? If anyone should like me it's surely the . . . wait! No! It wasn't anything. Must have been my imagination again. Still, I could have sworn I heard something . . . I did! I do! Again! It's sleigh bells.

"Help! Over here!" Kruge roared.

"Here! Help! Help! Over here!" The wind seemed to take his words and throw them back in his face.

He listened closer, heard the bells, definitely louder. Peering into the darkness and the driving snow, he could see nothing. But the sound was coming closer.

"Help! Over here!" As he shouted, he struggled to his feet.

Then suddenly, from only a few feet away, he heard a voice distinctly over the whistle of the wind. "What in the world are you doing up here alone?" The voice was gentle, but firm and possessed of authority.

Kruge could see nothing, but he moved cautiously in the direction of the voice. "Had an accident," he gasped. "My snowbuggy went over a cliff." He made out the side of what looked like a large sleigh. "Thought I was a goner for sure. Just about gave up hope."

"Climb aboard," said his benefactor. "You must be one of that bunch working down in the valley." It wasn't a question.

"More or less," said Kruge, climbing into the sleigh. He peered hard through the snow, trying to see the driver, but it was too thick to see more than an outline. The driver did appear to be large and warmly dressed. He handed Kruge a heavy blanket.

"Wrap up in this and settle back. We'll have you down in no time." With a flick of the reins the driver urged his team into motion. Smoothly, silently, they started down the mountain.

"How can you see where we're going?" he called above the wind. "I can't even see the tails of your horses."

The driver chuckled softly. "Oh, you get used to it when you spend as much time in the snow as I do," he said. "Mostly, though, it's the animals who know the way. Nothing else could possibly travel in this kind of weather. Don't worry. We'll get you down safely."

Kruge was impressed by the unassuming confidence. "I can't imagine what brought you out on a night like this," he said. "Surely any business could have waited until the storm was over."

The driver was silent for a moment. When he finally replied, his tone was slightly reproving. "Some things have to be done at a certain time, regardless of weather conditions or any other factors. This is true especially where people are concerned."

Kruge sensed that he was being lectured. Surprisingly enough, he felt the need to defend himself. "I've never broken my word in my life," he said. "I've given jobs to a lot of people too."

"Yes, providing a source of income for people is important," said the driver, "but how about their feelings? Have you made them feel like somebody? Have you let them maintain their respect and dignity? That too is important."

Maybe it was the experience he had just been through, maybe it was the fact that this man didn't know he was talking to *the* E.S. Kruge, but whatever the reason, Kruge listened and, for the first time in his adult life, even began considering.

After a bit he spoke. "Maybe you're right," he conceded. "Maybe that is important." It was a lot coming from Kruge. He put his head on the back of the seat. A million questions that he wanted to ask the driver flooded his mind, but he couldn't remember ever being so tired.

"That's right," said the driver. "Rest, and we'll have you down in no time."

The sleigh moved swiftly, surely and silently. Kruge couldn't even hear the sound of the horses' hooves. "Deep snow," he thought, "and I'd probably be under it, if it wasn't for this man." He fell asleep.

He was awakened by a tug on his sleeve. "Here we are," the voice of his rescuer said.

Kruge sat up straight. "Oh! Already?" He threw back the blanket and stepped to the snow-covered ground. "Why don't you come . . ." His voice trailed off as he looked at the driver, the sleigh, the animals, the blizzard, and he saw them all quite clearly.

"Think about some of the things I said." The driver flicked the reins and the sleigh moved away, leaving Kruge staring after it in silence.

He turned slowly and moved toward the building. Before he reached the door, it banged open.

"It's him!" shouted big Anders. "I told you I heard something!"

Kruge was swarmed over. Engulfed. Questions smothered him with concern.

"What happened?"

"Where were you?"

"We started up after you, but were practically blown off the mountain."

Kruge, poise regained, held up his hand. The magic was still there. Everyone grew quiet. Kruge addressed his pilot. "Kirby, I want you to find out what the weather's like back home." He motioned to the telephone.

As the pilot placed the call, Kruge moved to a window and stood looking out, silent, hands behind his back. The only sound in the room was that of the pilot's voice as he spoke on the telephone.

After a time the pilot put the phone in its cradle. "Clearing tonight, clear by morning," he said to Kruge's back.

Kruge turned from the window. "Fine!" he said jubilantly, clapping his hands together. He went to the phone and as he placed his call, everyone watched in silent curiosity.

A young female voice answered. "Hello?"

"Hello, Sue? This is Eb." He glanced at the listening men. "Listen, is the invitation to spend Christmas with you, Sumner and the kids still open?"

Surprise turned to pleasure. "Oh, will you? Can you? Please, please do!"

"You bet I will," Kruge said, fighting hard to control his cracking voice. "I'm out of town right now, but I'll be flying in tomorrow around—" he paused and glanced questioningly at his pilot.

Kirby thought for a minute. "By noon."

"I'll be in around noon tomorrow," Kruge finished telling Sue.

"That's wonderful!" she bubbled. "We'll be there to pick you up!"

She sounded genuinely delighted. Kruge felt good. "Fine, honey," he said, noticing and liking the sound of his own voice as he used alien words like *honey*. "And Sue—thank you very much."

"Oh, no," she protested. "Thank you, Eb. We *want* you with us! 'Bye. See you tomorrow."

Kruge replaced the phone and turned to the others. "Okay, here it is! Crockett, you're through! You'll fly back with me in the morning, but then you're finished."

Crockett looked at Kruge in confusion.

"Finished at the office, that is," Kruge said, breaking into a grin. "Didn't you say something about a son and Christmas?" He looked at the others. "Gentlemen, we're going to build Devil's Horn! More than that, we're going to make it the finest winter resort in the Western Hemisphere!" He put an arm around Crockett's shoulders. "Bob, here, is going to build it, and run it. Got to treat my good men right or else they might defect to the other side, wherever that is."

He laughed and so did the others, but above it all could be heard the faint tinkle of sleigh bells. Kruge walked to the window as the bells grew louder and louder, until finally they seemed to be just above the roof. Kruge looked at his watch, announcing softly, "It's midnight."

The bells began to recede.

Davenport finally managed to find his voice. Haltingly he asked, "How did you get down off that mountain?"

Kruge turned from the window, eyes twinkling, a smile of secret knowledge lighting his craggy features.

He surveyed the men for a moment, then slowly and deliberately, he winked.

A voice—soft and distant, yet clear and distinct—floated down to them. It said, of course, "Merry Christmas to all . . . and to all a good night!"

TWENTY-SIX HOURS TILL DAWN

Anonymous

Twenty-Six Hours Till Dawn

Anonymous

If a man on the street, offering prizes, would have walked up to the average American before November 24, 1971 and asked, "Where's Rahway?" his answer would probably have been a shoulder shrug or a simple "I don't know. Never heard of it." But if the same question had been asked the next day, as most people were settling down to the delicacies of their traditional Thanksgiving feast, the replies would have been quite different. By then, nearly every American who read the newspapers, watched television or listened to the radio, knew that Rahway was a small town situated in northern New Jersey. They were also aware of the fact that one of the state's major prisons sat on the outskirts of the tiny municipality and that behind the high stone walls another Attica seemed to be in the making.

NOVEMBER 24, APPROXIMATELY 9:15 P.M.: One minute the six hundred or so inmates from 1-wing and 4-wing were engrossed in a movie titled *Making It,* where a young high school student seemed bent on traveling through every bedroom in a Mesa, Arizona, suburb, and the next minute they were gaping at a huge hole in the screen. Someone had thrown a chair through it.

"You're all a bunch of punks if you don't put a stop to this bullshit!"

Everyone listened in stunned silence. In the back of the auditorium a sergeant moved to the phone. "We got a speechmaker up here, and a lot of guys are starting to crowd around."

"What about all them brothers up in Attica? Did they die for nothing? The same shit's going on here and we ain't doing a motherfucking thing about it!" Several inmates started for the exits. "That's right," the voice sneered. "If you ain't for real, get the fuck out!"

Warden U. Samuel Vukcevich acted promptly, and in an admirable, but foolhardy move, he wove his way past the prisoners who were streaming down the stairs on the 3-wing side of the auditorium. Chief Deputy Keeper Thomas Olden and three officers followed close on his heels.

The personal confrontation almost had the desired effect and in a moment, the warden and the speaker were locked in quiet conversation. Tensions began to ease and some guys started returning to the auditorium. Then, suddenly, someone yelled from the crowd that stood around the warden and the first speaker: "If you're jiving, motherfucker, just shut on up. If you're for real, let's get it on!"

All hell broke loose. Warden Vukcevich was grabbed and thrown to the floor. The chief and the other three officers tried to intervene and they too were seized, punched and wrestled down. It was only sheer good fortune that allowed Chief Olden to get clear of the melee and into the safety of the center, a barred enclosure directly under the auditorium that circled in front of each wing. But not so the three officers or the warden, and the punches and kicks came from every direction. Then a knife flashed and a man in the back cried, "Jesus Christ! They're going to get us all killed!"

The stampede was on and the auditorium shook as the remaining prisoners burst through the doors—nonparticipators just getting out of the way, as well as the emboldened rioters. Wing guards, who had been locking in the early stragglers from the movie, quickly secured their lock-boxes and fled behind the center doors. An officer in 4-Up found himself trapped on the top floor and had no recourse but to relinquish the keys, which fit the locks of the entire wing.

Amid cries of, "Remember Attica" and "We got Vukcevich," cell doors started swinging open. Those not yet released heard, yet few believed the sounds of smashing windows, crunching tables and chairs. By the time all cell doors were open and the door levers broken off, everyone realized that the riot was real!

Mop handles were broken in half and converted into clubs, padlocks were hooked onto the ends of belts or put into socks, home-made shivs appeared from a million and one stashes. Someone found a sledgehammer in one of the lock-boxes and led a band of convicts through the auditorium into 1-wing. There door locks were hammered off, first in 1-left, then in 1-right. On the top floor of 1-wing, those men confined to Administration Segregation were housed, as was the guard inside who never kept the keys to the heavy steel door. It had to be opened and closed from the outside. As prisoners started smashing at the brick wall, rather than attacking the heavy steel door, he phoned the center.

"They're trying to break in here," he cried in a panicstricken voice, trapped in the same cage with those residents considered incorrigible.

"Don't worry about it," came the reply from center. "Just sit tight. Your position is impregnable."

The Ad-Seg. guard watched chips fly off and bricks

215

begin to tumble in on the Ad-Seg. floor. "They're coming in," he said over the phone.

"Don't panic," came the calm reply. "They can't get to you."

The guard sighed heavily, hung up the phone and went to the cell of an inmate named Alfred Revenel, known to some as Quyyum.* He was known also for his honesty and his boldness. "Rev, don't let them hurt me!"

The officer had never been a bad sort, as officers go, and along with his other duties, he had to act as waiter/runner to the men in Ad-Seg., men who spent 90 percent of each day in their cells. A moment later enough bricks had tumbled inward for the besieging inmates to crash through and they rushed directly at the Ad-Seg. officer, their intentions of violence obvious.

"You punk-assed Uncle Tom motherfucker!"

"Leave him alone!" It was Revenel. "The guy's cool."

He was left alone and taken to 4-wing, where the other hostages were being held. A few moments later every door in Ad-Seg. had been busted open and the men freed.

Meanwhile, the 3-wing officer had managed to lock himself in the bathroom, and, on the way out, a lieutenant wisely slammed the door to the wing entrance, isolating 3-wing from the rioters. The same situation prevailed in 2-wing, but 1-wing and 4-wing were wide open and in control of the rioters.

Those who weren't armed found something, as roving bands began to run unchecked, setting fires, looting their fellow inmates' cells, spreading terror to those

* A few months ago Alfred Revenel escaped from a maximum security unit in Yardville and was subsequently shot down in a gun battle with policemen in Lancaster, Pennsylvania.

who refused to participate. Radios, typewriters, cigarettes, food, letters, photographs and other carefully hoarded momentoes of home were stolen or destroyed. In one instance, fourteen years of a man's life went up in flames.

Hoochmakers, afraid of being caught with the swag should the prison be stormed by troopers, dragged plastic-lined buckets and lockers out onto the tiers. Tomato wine, pineapple hooch and raisin jack, normally three packs a pint, was there for the taking. The sexual assaults were many and in 1-left, fifteen inmates took turns on a known homosexual, while in 1-right, three others dangled a young man over the third tier railing until he tearfully consented to their suggestions of degradation. In 4-Up, five men beat a youth unconscious and had their way with him.

For the most part, prisoners tried to stay close to their cells, but at times it was not possible due to smoking mattresses and burning wood and paint. On one occasion, the men in 4-Down were forced toward the center by smoke, then had to retreat back down the tiers again, as tear-gas bombs were shot in from the center. One man, weary from running back and forth, sat down in a puddle of murky water and started crying. He had been scheduled for a Thanksgiving furlough.

The first broadcast concerning the riot was heard around 10:30, and ill-informed sources reported that Warden Vukcevich had been killed in the initial outburst. It was also reported that state troopers were preparing to storm the prison. This gave even the most dissident prisoners pause and they moved to the street side of the prison to watch the developments. Sure enough, the parking lot was a beehive of activity as helmeted troopers armed themselves with shotguns, bullet-proof vests and ammunition. Other policemen pushed reporters, newscasters, cameramen and worried relatives out of the line of fire. The troopers moved into the administration building four abreast and a cold fear invaded the mind of every prisoner.

Barricades were hastily formed on tier landings and in doorways. Many inmates crawled under their beds, believing that a bullet had no way of knowing who "was" and who "wasn't."

The assault never came, and later it was revealed that the Ad-Seg. guard had been released after promising to try to stop the troopers from storming. He must have kept his word because they never did come.

During the next several hours an almost eerie quiet engulfed the besieged wings. The temperature dropped steadily and an icy wind had little difficulty getting in through the broken windows. The heat and water had long been turned off, and it was a common sight to see a teeth-chattering inmate with a blanket over his shoulders poncho-style or six and seven men huddled in one cell for warmth. A few made fires in their buckets and sat staring vacantly into the flames. Near daylight it started to rain.

Around dawn a helicopter clacked noisily over the prison and the rumor mill churned to life. "The governor is coming." But Governor Cahill was not coming to the prison and, instead, set up his headquarters at the nearby Woodbridge State School.

Since it just wouldn't do to have a riot without reasons, several factions made hasty attempts at organization. Runners were dispatched to all of the tiers, calling for a meeting in the auditorium. Some attended, some didn't, and amid broken parts of the movie projector and strips of film, the organizers themselves became targets of the disgruntled convicts.

"What about some food?"

"Who voted you guys into office anyway?"

"Riot, my ass! Negotiate, my balls! Somebody better

come up with my radio! It took me six months to save the money for it!"

"What about some water?"

Unable to satisfy anybody with any definite answers, the belated organizers soon found themselves alone, shaking their heads at each other.

Meanwhile, Archibald Alexander, chairman of the Prison Board of Managers, was talking at the center cage with the group that controlled the hostages. The self-appointed negotiators laid down "their" prerequisites for an end to the rebellion. Oddly enough, even these hastily thought-up grievances carried some merit. The final demand was contingent on reporters being allowed into the prison to personally hear the list of inmate grievances. After that the hostages would be released. Mr. Alexander asked to see the hostages to determine if they were all right, before relaying the information to the governor. After some deliberation, the junta agreed.

Warden Vukcevich was brought to the foot of the 4-Down stairs, supported by two inmates and with a blanket wrapped around his shoulders. The other hostages were also made visible, but were kept in the background. Mr. Alexander conversed at long range with the warden for a few moments and towards the end of the conversation, Warden Vukcevich raised his voice so that all could hear.

"I don't want these men hurt! I mean that! You're my boss and I'm telling you, if these men are hurt, I resign!" In the wake of a deafening applause, he was helped back to cell 7 on 4-tier, where he was being held.

By now hunger had added its misery to the lack of heat and water, and the jailhouse loan sharks did a brisk business. Many Thanksgiving dinners consisted of cold beans, spaghetti, peaches or fruit cocktail, at the cost of one pack per item. Peanut butter, tuna fish or potato chips could be had also, for two packs apiece. Many nervous men had smoked a week's supply of cigarettes during the night, but these too could be had, at the rate of two for three, seven for ten, ten for fifteen.

Mr. Alexander returned to the prison at about eight o'clock with the governor's reply: Three reporters would be let into the prison if the convicts would first release one of the hostages as a show of good faith. The committee agreed, no longer sure of their bargaining power due to the alienation of the inmates, who were concerned more with the protection of self and personal possessions. One guard was released without incident and soon after, the reporters arrived in the center, pads and pencils in hand. They listened to the list of complaints and departed at about ten P.M.

Then came the touchy part—the delivering of the hostages. There were still some with personal grudges and the like, but fortunately, someone had the foresight to provide an armed escort for the hostages. In several instances, weapons had to be brandished against splinter groups and individuals who still wished the warden harm.

Warden Vukcevich was the last one out, wounded, pale, sick, half supported by two inmates. Before he could take the final steps to safety, one inmate called to him from the third tier on 4-Down.

"I know you just said all that shit 'cause you were scared! You don't really give a fuck about us and nothing is ever going to change! Right after you get out, they'll come in whipping and shooting!"

The normal action would have been to dive the last few feet through the half-open center door, but during the last twenty-five-and-a-half hours, Warden Vukcevich hadn't been through anything that a normal man would experience. Perhaps he was indeed concerned, perhaps the fact that the "sleeping dragon" had finally

220

reared its head at Rahway caused him to take a real look at the people whose lives he controlled, for him it was something like a douche of ice-cold water. Whatever, he stopped and turned, still needing the support of the two inmates, and formed the word *no* with his mouth. He could muster no sound, though, so he shook his head emphatically from side to side. Then he sagged tiredly and had to be carried through the gate to freedom.

If anyone had any doubts about what came next, a voice over the loudspeaker quickly dispelled them. "It is requested at this time that each inmate return to his respective cell and remain there until the doors can be secured."

Tired, hungry, cold, scared, lungs filled with smoke, eyes watering from the tear-gas fumes, the prisoners shuffled back to their cells. Weapons were discarded anywhere, out windows, behind radiators, in trashcans, on the floor. Five minutes later, wary watchers saw the first of the blue uniforms on the tier landings. A short time later, makeshift repairs were performed on the lock-boxes and the doors began slamming shut with a banging finality. The riot was over.

NORMAN A. PORTER

Massachusetts State Prison, Norfolk, Massachusetts

Norman spent his first twenty-eight years tearing up the New England turf, then dug in and at present seems bent on patching it up again. Since his incarceration in 1961, he has achieved too much to mention in a biographical sketch. Some of his accomplishments include eight correspondence courses and college credits in sociology, American history, creative writing, American literature, drama, economics, Spanish and accounting. He has made numerous appearances on radio and television and was a prime instrument, via the Norfolk Information Committee, in the revolutionary approach to prisons in Massachusetts. Through all of this, he still manages to function as editor of the prison paper, vice-chairman of The Lifers' Group, Inmate Council member, Debating Society chairman, *Time* Magazine class instructor and Quiz Club coach. Talk about putting time to work!

Greater Prison

Norman A. Porter

I got up early this morning
tired from laying in bed
sleepless in the night of boredom
tossing covers off frantically
as if they were chains
crisscrossing my body
binding me for life to prison
snapping locks on the prime of my youth
dictating my mind to passion
—the passion of revenge—
of a far greater prison
than this one of stone walls and iron cages
restless to the world in short supply
seconds go by slower than hours
hours slower than days
days slower than weeks
weeks slower than months
months slower than years
years slower than decades.

And the minutes to write this
seem like eternity

stored, pent-up energy
keeping me awake
denying me the escape narcotic sleep
the last refuge for a mind on guard
against the slaughter of self-respect
as the man goes through his key ring
to find the one for my mind
to open it and offer up as proof
the rage he provokes to justify
the way he treats me.

Most men want to be
what they're expected to be
how else do we win approval
and feel ourselves members of the race
than to serve a need for another's existence
men cannot live without women
screws cannot live without convicts
who can judge a person
bad or good
if we didn't have ministers
to judge good by
if we didn't have convicts
to judge bad by.

I'm helpless here to serve that need
for if I turned good
then each of us would have to face
the mirror of our own makeup
where good and bad are blended
some more good, some more bad
and we judge the difference
by what we fear
by what we admire
standards that do not balance
for in fearing we deny what can be
for in admiring we deny what is

we go on secure in our knowledge
that we are right in our distinctions
and use that right
as comfort on lonely winter nights
to order our lives
the best of all possible worlds
each choice built on yesterday's mistakes
experience called wisdom in later life
when we've discovered we've passed ourselves by.

We've each all chosen prison
rigid lives unmovable as the wall
locking ourselves into cages
that contain our energies
in a space as small as my cell.

The Guy I Killed

Norman A. Porter

I remember the guy I killed
I drank with him once
down the Lynn Tap & Grill

God, it doesn't seem real at all
like it never happened
but it did, I know it did.

I can't always remember
all of that night
blocked out of my mind
during the time the gun went off
couldn't have been more than a minute
that scene is like a bad frame in a horror movie.

Each time I play that movie
I speed the camera up
and go right by the whole thing.

But still I've come to that point in my life
where I don't want justification
   or even that elusive legal justice

—just want to be forgiven—
I remember the guy I killed
wow, it seems so long ago.

It's been ten years now
since that rainy Friday night
when my crime partner and I
ran headlong into Robert Hall's
like madmen of long ago
with porkpie hats and bandanas
sawed-off shotguns and silver-plated pistols.

It was the money we were after
Nobody, nobody was supposed to die.

Who ever thought there would be heroes there?

Guns went off.

People jumping on people.

Just once—for a brief second—
did it flash through my head
that all was madness
—couldn't really be happening—

It pains me every time I remember that second.

I see the guy I killed
I drank with him once
down the Lynn Tap & Grill.

We got away that night
but they caught the guy driving the car
—a nice brand-new four-door Buick,
I stole over in front of the Lafayette House—

He just couldn't wait to tell all he knew,
soon the Police were after us.
We wound up getting caught,
—and pleading guilty to murder and robbery
to spare the horrors of the electric chair—

I remember the guy I killed.
I wonder if I had died
from charges of electricity
would the state remember the guy they killed.

Nonetheless, here we are ten years later
my crime partner (not the one driving the car) and I.
He lives two cell blocks over
from my cluttered little cell.

I've lived every minute
of every day
of every year
whether I've wanted to or not
with that one bad frame
staring me right in the face.

I remember the guy I killed
I drank with him once
down the Lynn Tap & Grill.

I guess I will always remember him
even long after
any day which might come
when they let me go.

Addendum—a year and a half later
Tonight,
I now know how
the friends

of the guy I killed
must have felt.
For tonight
my crime partner
got killed
in his cell block——a few over from mine——
11 and a half years later.

Death Row

Norman A. Porter

I know a guy that people say
killed a cop in a shoot-out
after a bank robbery.

He's on death row now;
it's been close to eleven years
since the electrically operated
barred door slid shut on him.

I wonder how he feels
just being there all this time.
I'll bet it really must hurt
—that is if he still has his sanity.

I know that guy;
knew him before he went on the row
—knew what he once was.
Now that he's been on the row so long
he no longer is
what he once was.
He probably needs glasses

eyes go bad when they're not used
to see beyond five feet in any one direction.

I wonder what he does for excitement
—shout dirty words at the screws
who can't pinch him anymore.

Or play chess by number
with the death-condemned convict
in the cell two cells down from him
whom he's never seen
—for nine years he's known him only as a voice.

Or maybe chase cockroaches
round and round his cell
(who said cockroaches survive only where there is wood)
making thimble chariots
drawn by four albino cockroaches
across his no-seat toilet bowl
—what else is there to do?

I wonder if he thinks anybody cares for him
Christmas cards returned to sender
all ripped open and pried apart
because they didn't come from a relative.

I wonder if the cop he killed
suffered the pain for being killed
that he suffers now for having killed him.

He's died a thousand deaths, a thousand days,
his execution date is X'ed on the calendar.

Can we kill a man a thousand times
while he still breathes
feeling our mercy naked in overalls
scant protection from the weight of our numbers.

I know that man on death row.
I've cried in my bed for him at times
not because I feel sorry for him
because I feel sorry for myself.

How many times have I locked people away
from me and kept them far
for fear their poison would come to me.
I put them in prison and imprisoned myself.

How many times have I
given people the silent treatment
like they didn't exist.

Death row is the silent treatment
I know that man there
I wonder if he knows I think of him.

Frozen Steel Bars

Norman A. Porter

The frozen steel bars
crowd my face
as so many vertical strips
of hacksaw-proof metal
that go into forming four sides
of a cage that is my cell
and contains me like a wasted rat
for none to see
except for others caged like me
and myrmidons hired to cage us
yet we all know
prisons, exist as justifiable existence
to keep some rats from being wasted.

The bars are placed so tight together
that my vision blurs
and I see only between one-inch bars
half-inch slits of the world beyond.

Being kept thus imprisoned
we see less and less as our eyes atrophy
and become accustomed to only being needed

to see inside the 4 foot by 10 foot cage
like we're all albino Mexican cave fish.

But that's not all that shrinks and diminishes
as a real live human
goes from needing and using every full body function
to a caged wasted rat
with bed, toilet and sink all touching each other
and the mind malfunctions in order to adjust
to eating, sleeping, excreting, washing and having sex
all within a distance not further than 2 feet from each act
in controlled minimum quantity whose only standard
is to sustain the caged at barest level
then our behavior adapts
and rationalizes away our treasured worth
to escape the owners of self-destruction
that surely comes with asserting humaneness
and demanding treatment worthy of such.

The cagers bear down as proof
with each docile broken prisoner
that a lesson's been learned.

The cages are kept shut till rusted
from years of containing those to be taught
the lesson over and over and over and over again
till the results and effects of those who cage
are seen in sadistic ejaculation of more time, more time
and the good public body wipes the wetness
from its judicial-correctional fly.

Alas, for in the end the cagers cage themselves
by providing a surefire method to insure
that crooks will exist to loot and plunder again
and the cage they build for themselves
through law, custom and belief

is just as confining, restrictive and destroying
as the one made of frozen steel bars.

So who wins in the end
the cagemakers
or those inside
the answer is found
in who's hurt by a crime
who's hurt from being caged
for those of us who can't see
from eyes clouded with getting even
it doesn't matter who gets hurt
we go on making cages
and being locked inside.

FRANK EARL ANDREWS

Rahway State Prison, Rahway, New Jersey

Frank has spent twenty-seven of his thirty-six years under supervision of some sort, beginning with the New Jersey State Home For Boys, at age nine. In 1962 he staged a rather unique escape and for his efforts received a unique prison sentence—fifty-five to sixty-seven years. For five years he stayed in and out of trouble with the prison authorities, but one day he looked around and realized that his time was doing him and not vice versa. He tried his hand at creative writing and to his amazement sold his first article. Since that time he hasn't looked back and his crowning achievement came two years ago when he co-authored, co-edited, co-promoted and co-published an anthology of convict fiction titled *Voices from the Big House.* Believing that a busy mind makes a free soul, Frank is currently working on two separate books at the same time; one which is an autobiography of his life and another which he terms "earthshaking and a labor of love." He hopes one day to be free, but likens his situation to that of the little boy who falsely alarmed villagers by crying wolf.

Massacre at Cortez

Frank Earl Andrews

Like a smooth-shelled water bug skittering across a pond, the black El D zipped along the desert floor. Johnny Hammond drove, hunched forward, his brown knuckles almost white where he gripped the wheel. Between furtive glances in the rear-view mirror, he coaxed the black machine on, crooning to it, as if the two hundred fifty-horsepower engine would respond to the urgency of his voice.

George Corson sat alongside, his rugged face expressionless. Between his feet sat a black valise holding twenty-five thousand dollars. It was blood money, having been exchanged for the lives of three bank tellers and a guard. George touched the barrel of the Thompson sub bridging the gap between his knees, still warm though he hadn't used it for almost a half hour. He checked his watch. Fifteen minutes ago they had crossed the Nevada state line into California.

"Where the hell's the turnoff!" Johnny's voice was high-pitched.

George allowed himself a thin smile. "Relax. When we get there, you'll see it."

"We should have reached it by now!"

George glanced at the kid, his movements, the beads of sweat on his forehead. Johnny was scared shitless, but his fear must not have been conveyed to his hands because they guided the car deeper into the Mojave with calm precision.

"Just drive. We'll make it."

Johnny wanted to scream at the white killer's coolness, but he remembered the people at the bank, the way they had danced to the melody of George's stuttering machine gun. No, he had no intention of making him mad.

The turnoff they looked for was nothing more than a set of deeply rutted tracks, leading off the highway to Cortez, a ghost town of some fame in the late 1800s. George spied it first.

"There."

Johnny jammed the brake pedal, causing the Caddy to skid in a half circle, then floored the accelerator. The rear wheels spun on the pavement for a moment, then caught with a screech and the El D shot off the highway, swerving from side to side as the tires bounced in and out of the age-old furrows. A cloud of red dust mushroomed up behind them. George checked his watch. Twenty minutes since they had crossed the state line. They were making good time.

The trail sloped upward and Johnny had to constantly fight the wheel. He was glad of the need to concentrate on something, anything to give his troubled mind respite from the gory scene at the bank, anything to drown out the sounds and sights of humans twitching and crying in pools of their own blood. It also helped him forget the gas chamber and the fact that, if caught, he would be sitting right alongside George Corson. He cursed the white gunman for the hundredth time, but not out loud. . . .

Two weeks ago he'd been the pride of the southern stock circuit, just winning the Elkton 200 and a neat four hundred fifty dollars. At a black jump joint right outside of Baltimore, George Corson walked into his life. Dressed in an immaculate sharkskin suit, he looked around the Crippled Monkey like he owned the place, even though it was a hangout for black folks. His hard face reflected amusement, as he watched a group of young bloods bounce around to a funky James Brown side. Johnny was impressed and it suddenly seemed important that he disassociate himself from the younger set.

"Waste of good energy, huh?"

George Corson shrugged. "Good exercise." The bartender brought him a drink. "You drive pretty good."

Johnny was proud of the win. "Pulled down almost five hundred."

George shook his head. "Small stuff," he said, sipping his drink, smacking his lips, "considering the risks."

"What do you call big stuff?" Johnny asked, miffed.

"Ten, fifteen thousand. . . . You could make that much."

Johnny never had more than five hundred dollars in his pocket at one time, and he had enough sense to realize that his dreams of Indy and Darlington were just that—dreams. A man needed to know somebody, he needed some good wheels under him, he needed to be white. With fifteen thousand dollars, he could have all of this, be his own man. That kind of money would buy a winning machine.

"Who do I have to rob?" He grinned, meaning it as a joke.

"A bank," George said easily.

Johnny's grin faded. For a moment he thought the white man toyed with him, but as he studied the

243

granite face, the expressionless eyes, he knew he'd heard right. He fingered the money in his pocket, enough for a few days of partying, then back to begging for a job, the grease, the sweat, the risks, the empty days between victories, the chump change he got when he finally did come out on top.

At the sight of the narrow wooden bridge up ahead, some of the tension left him. Everything had gone according to plan. Cortez wasn't far away. They would hide the car and hole up. The cops would never think anyone foolish enough to turn off into the desert. After a while they would take down their roadblocks, figuring the bank robbers had slipped through.

The tires rolled onto the weathered bridge with a clatter and Johnny eased up on the accelerator. Halfway across disaster struck, and ancient floorboards squeaked, splintered and collapsed. The Caddy dropped nose-first into a shallow riverbed, roaring, rending, as metal grated on wood, tearing the roof, scraping the sides. Johnny saw a bridge support rushing at his head and threw himself to one side. The last thing he remembered was the giant timber smashing through the windshield.

George Corson opened his eyes. There was nothing but murk and for an instant he experienced pure terror. Then a dull throbbing started in his head and he heaved a sigh of relief. Dead people didn't have headaches. He waited until his throbbing head stopped spinning, then fished around in the glove compartment for a flashlight. The door on the driver's side had sprung open and in the place where Johnny Hammond had been sitting, a thick wooden beam impaled the El D. George found the Thompson sub halfway under the seat and after several attempts at opening the door on his side, slid under the timber and out the other side.

He played the light along the ground until he located

244

Johnny Hammond's motionless form. Blood stained the side of his head and his neck was twisted at an odd angle. He appeared to be dead and George thought about that for a minute. Maybe the accident had saved him some trouble. A short burst from the machine gun lit up the night, flopping Johnny's body a few feet further along the dried riverbed.

George dragged the corpse to the car, worked open a back door and dumped the kid into the back seat. He thought about burning the Caddy, but decided against it because the car was nearly covered by the bridge wreckage. A fire might only serve as a beacon. Besides, if the fuzz found the turnoff, they would find the car, burnt or not. He pulled an army surplus knapsack from under Johnny's body and tossed away everything but a canteen of water and half a dozen clips of ammunition. He lined these around his waist. By the time he climbed out of the gulley, the sun had started its daily climb. He checked his watch and cursed. Five forty-five. They'd been sitting under that goddamn bridge for almost thirteen hours.

A lizard panted in the shade of a huge boulder, pitted by years of wind until it looked like a giant sponge. When the man stopped a few feet away, the reptile changed colors. The two remained motionless, comrades sharing the same relief from the terrible heat. After a while George moved out across a sea of lava. Blood and dirt caked his face, while the sun blistered him, cracked his lips, parched his throat. As he moved his dragging feet made ragged lines on the desert floor and his breathing came in gulping gasps. Finally he fell, and the last of the water failed to rejuvenate him enough to rise.

It seemed an eternity before he crawled out of the lava bed and clawed his way to the top of a rocky hill. Bleary-eyed, he stared at the valley below and broke into a fit of manic laughter. Swarms of screaming Indians circled Cortez, pouring arrows and lances into the cluster of clapboard buildings. His laughter turned into dry-wracked sobbing.

Cortez's one claim to fame was that it had once been the site of a furious Indian battle. Silver had been the town's original attraction, but the strike was short-lived and swarms of fortune hunters left as quickly as they had come. Apaches, who had been driven back into the Sierra Nevada, came out of the hills, attacking what they thought was a sitting duck. The legend had it that they got more than they bargained for. Now, some frigging movie outfit wanted to reenact the battle.

"We can't go back!" George shouted to nobody. Then realizing that he was alone, he answered. "Damn right we can't." He gained his feet and stumbled down the hill.

Some of the braves saw him and detached themselves from the main group. George laughed deliriously as they thundered his way. He roared when their feathered arrows whistled past his head. "They think we're part of the show!" he yelled to nobody. "Hah hah hah haaaaaaa. . . ." A lance buried itself in the fleshy part of his thigh and tumbled him to his knees. "What the hell . . ."

For a frantic instant his mind sought an explanation, but the torment in his leg wiped away any attempt to search for rationale, and left only room for thoughts of retribution. He fired from a sitting position and his sputtering Thompson dealt death to four of the greasy marauders. Two others reined in hard and rode back out of range.

Reinforcements soon joined the two who had halted, and after a wary conference, a wild screech started them at George again. An arrow pierced his chest and brought an involuntary cry from his cleft lips. Savagely he wrenched the lance from his leg and broke in half the shaft of the arrow that protruded from his chest. With an animal snarl, he struggled up, a sickly grin on his hard face. It was time these bastards found out they had bitten into the wrong cupcake. He waited until they were almost on him, then squeezed the trigger, cutting a swath in the red mass twenty feet across.

The townspeople came alive and between them they effected a withering cross fire. Everywhere, painted bodies littered the ground, while cries of dying humans and wounded animals added to the sounds of gunfire and pounding hooves. The riders that fled for the foothills of the Sierra Nevada were few in number.

After the silence of the desert took over again, George made a feeble move toward Cortez, and fell on his face. He began to crawl, wondering why no one came out to help him. Hadn't he helped them? Yet had he? There were no hostile Indians anymore. Then whom had he been shooting at? What of the stinking flesh surrounding him now, the blood bubbling red from his leg? Why the crude arrow tearing his insides apart?

He used the last of his strength to pull himself over a wagon tongue and somersaulted into the dirt of Cortez's single street. For a time he rested on his back, grimacing at the sky, a passive cerulean. Through the fog of agony he tried to make some sense of the recent happenings. He thought vaguely of the black valise and that he'd left it at the Caddy. The thought didn't disturb him unduly.

A circle of peering faces formed above. He knew them all, the bank guard sporting half a face, the tellers, their clothes full of holes and splotched with blood. He even saw Johnny Hammond, coagulated blood and grime smearing the side of his head.

"We can use his gun when they attack again," Johnny said through a mist. "That honky's good with that gun. . . ."

Ultimate understanding came to George then, but when it did, he took it calmly. He was cool about most things, even this. He rolled his head sideways and looked at the dusty face of his watch. It showed five forty-five, and always would. . . .

Last Stand

Frank Earl Andrews

They lay together, and the ground didn't seem so cold or hard. They'd been together five months, beginning with her first day at the mountain outpost. He was twenty years old, she only nineteen. She was the only woman there. The others had all surrendered to the enemy.

Several hundred feet away lay the rest of the men, asleep in sandbag-reinforced dugouts and trenches. In front of them sprawled a valley, though it was now hidden by the night except for occasional flashes from the enemy gun muzzles, as giant shells were lobbed at the mountain top. The sporadic artillery assault was designed more for an unsettling effect than anything else because most of the missiles exploded far down the slope or whistled by high overhead. The weary men slept, anyway, or lay silent, each locked into his own thoughts. No one could say just when the final attack would take place, but it would probably come at dawn.

She moved closer to him and kissed his ear. She thought some about the forthcoming battle, but most of her thoughts centered around the baby inside her body.

"At night sometimes, I dream that this is only a silly game and that we can jump up when we are tired of playing and say 'I quit! Go home!' Can you imagine the sun rising in the morning with the war being over?"

"It *will* be over in the morning," he said grimly, "but we'll make it expensive for them."

She sighed and her breath fluttered against his neck. "I wish there was some way we could escape all of this." She wanted to tell him of his child, yet realized that it would only make things more difficult for him.

"If anyone could escape, none of us would be here now." His tone was one of resignation.

"Why doesn't the colonel surrender?" she rationalized out loud. "Surely life under foreign rule would be better than no life at all."

He cursed under his breath the stupid politicians who had pushed for and formulated the international ban on nuclear weaponry. It was like the heavyweight champion of the world relinquishing his knockout punch, making him just another fighter.

"I'd rather die first!" he hissed, probably reflecting the colonel's views on the idea as well.

"There must be something we can do, besides sit here and wait to die." She wanted so badly to give her child a chance to live, yet refused to leave her man alone to face the horrors of dying.

He turned on his side to face her, brushed her hair with his fingertips. "There is . . . make the most of what we have left. . . ."

She snuggled closer, kissed the stubble on his chin, enjoying the feel of it, as it tickled and scratched her lips. He wrapped his windbreaker around them both.

"Be careful! You'll crush us!"

For a moment the significance of her words slipped

past unnoticed. Then it dawned on him what she had said and he sat up.

"What do you mean *us?*"

She hadn't meant to let him know, but by thinking in the plural sense for so long, the words had come out inadvertently. She turned away, buried her face in her sleeve and began to weep quietly.

For a moment he watched her trembling silhouette. His anger quickly subsided and he leaned over her, turning her face so that he could kiss her lips, her forehead, her eyes, the salt tears.

"Perhaps we can get you out. I'll see the colonel."

"Be quiet," she whispered. She put her cheek to his and licked the lobe of an ear. "I hope the baby won't be as stubborn as you." She laughed, but her breathing, so familiar, told him how troubled she really was. "What will we name her?" she asked, for the moment forgetful of their present plight.

He chuckled. "How do you know it will be a her?"

She giggled. "All right, if it's a boy you can name him. If it's a girl, I have the final say."

"Izzza deal." He laughed and gave her a sloppy kiss on the neck.

"What would you name our baby, if it was a boy?"

"Hmmmmmm. . . ." He puckered his lips in thought. "I would name him Napoleon Caesar," he said presently. "I would make him a king before he took his first steps."

"And if it's a girl, I will call her Czarina Maharani and make her a princess," she said, caught up with the idea.

Cold reality returned and they both grew silent again. He was the first to speak. "Things have changed. You must escape."

She smiled sadly. "The only way would be to surrender. I won't do that unless you come with me."

"Impossible! Only a coward would desert his country!"

"*Fool* would be a better word!" she retorted. "What good is there in dying, bravely or otherwise? Besides, in this case the dying will be for nothing. There's no country left to die for."

He shook his head. "I couldn't live with myself."

"Then, perhaps the *three* of us dying is the only answer." She spoke dully, but realized that she was applying pressure on him now. Yet a child needed both a mother and a father, and with the way things were going to be when the sun rose in the morning, it would need one more than ever. "When they come tomorrow, the three of us will die right here."

He said no more. Later they rose. He took her hand and they climbed higher, to the very top of the mountain. It was said that a person could see four states from where they stood, but in the predawn haze they had trouble even distinguishing the headlights of the enemy vehicles, as they moved up troops and supplies, contemptuous of the ragged remnants that waited for them.

The sun rose mercilessly, pure and bright in a sky clear blue, but tinged by smoke clouds that billowed up around Asheville and Chattanooga, on the Tennessee side.

The planes came first, bombing and strafing the mountain top, then the artillery increased tenfold and continued to bang away for a solid hour. When the enemy forces started up the slopes, what was left of the once most powerful military host in the world, dug in around the perimeter for its last stand. No one even noticed that the young man and woman were not in their places.

Muhammad Ali—In the Joint!

Frank Earl Andrews

There's a lot more to Muhammad Ali than the composition of slick poems about his ring opponents, a crisp left hook or the "Ali Shuffle." He displayed that when he strolled into Rahway State Prison in New Jersey, scene of the now-infamous Thanksgiving Riot back in 1971.

It was a startled group of prisoners, lying in their cells during the afternoon count period, who heard the voice of the former heavyweight champion crackle over the institutional loudspeaker system: "First, I'd like to say hello to my brothers and my fans. Next, to those who root for the other guy . . ."

Amid ripples of laughter, inmates jumped to their cell doors and an enjoyable fifteen minutes ensued, with Ali relating his plans for knocking George Foreman's shoes off. Faces and ears stuck through the bars and there were grins and giggles as Ali called the shots: "If I don't jive—he'll go in five. If I take my time—he'll go in nine. Maybe three—if he aggravates me."

A mouse could be heard peeing on cotton when the heavyweight told the prisoners that he was en route to New York, where he planned to sign a contract that very night. Ali then met with an old boxing friend, Rubin "Hurricane" Carter, following up a promise made on the Johnny Carson Show a few weeks earlier. He told the beleaguered ex-middleweight contender, who has been fighting a seven-year knockdown, drag-out battle with the courts, that he would elicit support everywhere he went in an effort to help overturn Rubin's triple-life conviction. Ali added with a chuckle, "I have an idea what you are going through. I did seven days and almost died!"

When the count cleared the usually somber "Hurricane" sauntered into 3-wing, sporting a grin a yard wide. As he passed my cell I couldn't help commenting, "Watcha grinning like a chessy cat about?"

Rubin's smile broadened and it made him look good. I had known him since we were kids in the Jamesburg State Home for Boys and I don't remember ever seeing him smile like that. "Just got done talking to an old friend," he told me.

"Is he going to help you?" I asked.

"Yup," Rubin replied smugly.

I thought back to 1966, when Rubin came into Trenton State Prison, toting a triple-life sentence for the alleged slaying of three people in a Paterson, New Jersey, tavern. He locked on the tier over me and I remember hearing the tack-tack-tack, as he typed all day and into the wee hours of the night, preparing legal briefs and writing his autobiography, *The Sixteenth Round,* which is scheduled for publication by Viking Press in July. I was still thinking of these and other things, and wishing there was something I could do to help the "Hurricane" up off the canvas, when the bell rang for mess.

"How did Ali sound?" I asked Rubin, as my door swung open.

"For real," Rubin answered.

"You feel good, huh?"

"Like I just had a cool drink from a mountain stream."

"Going to eat?"

Rubin laughed. "Ain't got to eat no more." He faked a left hook at my head and walked down the tier.

VIKKI

We Ain't Telling!

Vikki has never been incarcerated and never will be! She met editor Frank Earl Andrews two years ago through a wire-mesh screen, and the seeds of "Love Story" were planted. Vikki is seven years old, out of sight and too young to dig it yet!

Jan 12 1973

Dear Frank Hi Frank
I like you very
very very much

Frank, what Do you
think of that Frank E.A.
Dear Do you like
me Frank ? , will you
write me ?
will you please Deer
Frank will you please
please Frank please

I know Frank I know
you I think I do.
Love Vikki
to Frank

JOHN W. SELLERS

John spends five days and two nights each week behind bars, but he is not a prisoner. He teaches art at Rahway State Prison and along with his natural talents holds some heavy credentials, including a B.S. in art education from Penn State University. His future plans are to obtain a graduate degree in the fine arts and to continue working within the prison system, in an effort to draw out as much of the locked-away talent and creativity as he can find. John is twenty-four years old, married and is the father of two dynamite little peeps. He gets along fabulously with prisoners, not an easy task, but it isn't hard to figure out why—along with being an artist deluxe, John Sellers is a human deluxe.

STEVE HERINGES

Steve is a student teacher from Keene College in New Jersey, who came to Rahway State Prison to pick up some field credits under John W. Sellers, our wacky art teacher. Steve is married, thirty-one years old and has one child. I don't know if Steve picked up much at Rahway in the line of fine arts and education, but I do know he was "hanging out" like a champ, just naturally liking folks and being liked.

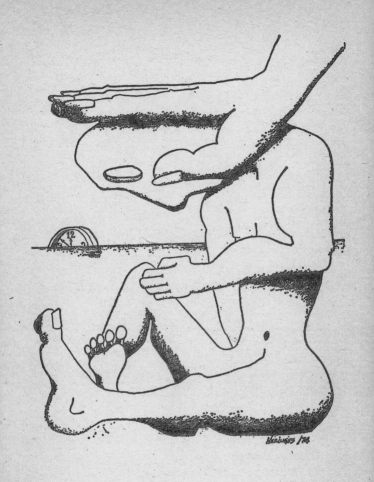

Steve Hammers 8/72

Material That Appeared in

Inmate Papers

THE CLARION—California Institution for Women
    Passing Time Away
    A Turtle's Tale
ENCHANTED NEWS—New Mexico State Penitentiary
    Little Brother Mad
    Another Christmas Carol
FYSK—Virginia State Penitentiary
    I Wish I Were a Unicorn
THE FORTUNE NEWS—The Fortune Society—New
  York
    Would You Be Normal?

Excitement Reading

P18

are you missing out on some great Pyramid books?

You can have any title in print at Pyramid delivered right to your door! To receive your Pyramid Paperback Catalog, fill in the label below (use a ball point pen please) and mail to Pyramid...